CONTEMPORARY ISSUES IN MEDICAL LAW

Eduardo Vasconcelos dos Santos Dantas
Marianna Chaves

CONTEMPORARY ISSUES IN MEDICAL LAW

GZ EDITORA

Rio de Janeiro
2018

1ª edição – 2018

Capa
Marcella Real

CIP-Brasil. Catalogação-na-fonte.
Sindicato Nacional dos Editores de Livros, RJ.

D211c

Dantas, Eduardo Vasconcelos dos Santos
Contemporary issues in medical law / Eduardo Vasconcelos dos Santos Dantas, Marianna Chaves. - 1. ed. - Rio de Janeiro : LMJ Mundo Jurídico, 2017.
214 p.; 23 cm.

Inclui bibliografia e índice
ISBN 978-85-9524-029-2

1. Responsabilidade (Direito) - Brasil. 2. Médico e paciente. I. Chaves, Marianna. II. Título.

17-45894 CDU: 347.51:61

contato@editoragz.com.br
www.editoragz.com.br

Av. Erasmo Braga, 299 - sala 202 - 2º andar – Centro
CEP: 20020-000 – Rio de Janeiro – RJ
Tels.: (0XX21) 2240-1406 / 2240-1416 – Fax: (0XX21) 2240-1511

Impresso no Brasil
Printed in Brazil

"To achieve great things, two things are needed;
a plan, and not quite enough time."

Leonard Bernstein

About the Authors

Eduardo Vasconcelos dos Santos Dantas
Lawyer, licensed to practice in Brazil (since 1995) and Portugal (since 2011); Specialist in Consumer Law by the University of Castilla-La Mancha, Spain; LL.M. in Medical Law by the University of Glasgow, Scotland; PhD Candidate in Civil Law –University of Coimbra, Portugal; Former Vice-President and member of the Board of Governors of the World Association for Medical Law; Vice-President of the Asociación Latinoamericana de Derecho Médico; Member of the International Advisory Board of the Observatory on Human Righs : Bioethics, Health and Environment, of the University of Salerno, Italy; Member of the Association de Recherche et de Formation en Droit Médical; Vice-President of the Bioethics and Biolaw Comission of the Brazilian Institute of Family Law – IBDFAM; Author of several articles published in Brazil, Portugal, Israel, USA, Poland, Mexico, Czech Republic and France; Author of the books Direito Médico (Editora GZ, 2009), Comentários ao Código de Ética Médica (Editora GZ, 2010), Droit Médical au Brésil (Editora GZ, 2013); and Aspectos Jurídicos da Reprodução Humana Assistida (Editora GZ, 2018); Member of the Special Commission of Medical Law in the Federal Council of the Brazilian BAR.
E-mail: eduardodantas@eduardodantas.adv.br

Marianna Chaves
PhD Candidate in Civil Law – University of Coimbra, Portugal; Master of Laws – University of Lisbon; Post-Graduated in Informed Consent – Centre for Biomedical Law – University of Coimbra; Post-Graduated in Medical Law and Bioethics – University of Lisbon; Post-Graduated in Reproduction Law – Centre for Biomedical Law – University of Coimbra; Member of the World Association for Medical Law; Member of the International Society of Family Law; President of the Bioethics and Biolaw Comission of the Brazilian Institute of Family Law – IBDFAM; Member of the LGBTI Rights Comittee of the Federal Council of Brazilian BAR; Attorney at Law registered at the Brazilian BAR since 2007; Legal Consultant and Researcher.
E-mail: mariannachaves@eduardodantas.adv.br

Table of Contents

VII
Advance Directives: The consecration of autonomy and dignity of the human being *(Marianna Chaves)*

VIII
Coming Home with a baby from Brazil: How to advise U.S. intended parents who go abroad to have children through ART. *(Marianna Chaves)*

IX
Gestational Surrogacy in Portugal and Brazil. *(Marianna Chaves)*

X
Brief notes on the surplus embryos. *(Marianna Chaves)*

XI
Test-tube families: Brief remarks on legal limits to ART in Brazil. *(Marianna Chaves)*

Presentation

> *"You will soon be 82. You have shrunk six centimetres and you weigh just 45 kilos and you are still beautiful, gracious and desirable,' it begins. 'It is now 58 years that we have lived together and I love you more than ever,' he wrote. 'I carry in myself a devouring emptiness within the hollow of my chest, which can only be filled by the warmth of your body against mine. 'Sometimes, at night, I see the silhouette of a man walking behind a hearse along an empty road in a deserted landscape,' wrote Gorz. 'I am that man. I don't want to attend your cremation, I don't want to receive your ashes in a bowl"* (In Gorz, André. **Lettré à D.: histoire d'um amour)**[1].

CONTEMPORARY ISSUES IN MEDICAL LAW treats about a new intriguing frontier of law. Eduardo Vasconcelos dos Santos Dantas e Marianna de Almeida Chaves Pereira Lima establish a sophisticated dialogue between new issues that, derived from new medical techniques, were imposed on jurists in an environment that suggests a potential resumption of tension and adjustments between laws and the human will, individually considered.

It is possible to infer, with a great margin of certainty, that we are facing a new beginning of a era of cooperation between the various contours that medicine and law, dissociated, gave to ethics.

Discussing the issues put here is a great action of responsibility in the face of the current urgencies described by each of the chapters that the reader has before them. Also, is to understand the human, social, political and moral dimensions that derive from the knew techniques and medical practices in situations that challenge the limits once known to medicine.

Based on a well-founded consensus - that one of the current pillars of the relationship between doctors and patients is rediscovered in the duty to inform2 - the

---

1 After living 58 years together, Andre Gorz, one of the greatest social and political thinkers of the twentieth century, prefaced by Sartre, decided, with his wife Dorine, to suspend all the medical efforts applied for decades to her condition. They died together, at home, on September 22, 2007

2 DANTAS, Eduardo. **Droit Médical au Brésil**: Essais et Reflexions sous la Perspective du Droit Comparé. Rio de Janeiro: GZ Editora, 2013, p. 5. Free translation. In the original: "*Um des piliers actuels de la relation médecin – patient*

authors orchestrate themes of high complexity, using both the method that rescues the historical experiences of medical practice, and the systematic method, alerting the reader to the incovenience of interpretation and application of law in isolation.

In the beginning, Eduardo contextualizes the hole of patient's autonomy in the brazilian experience. After briefly recalling the understanding in the end of life situations, he already exposes one of the two central problems faced in this book: the systems of medical self-regulation and the resumption of the condition of being endowed with autonomy by the patient.

In dealing with the questions of the patient's choice raised by the referring active role of the Federal Council of Medicine, they adopted a two-step approach, which requires a careful reading of the arguments put forward.

Tensioning the proper duties of medicine, conditioned to medical ethics, and the personal rights of patients, we have here demonstrated the difficulty of finding a margin that guarantees balance, both to doctors and lawyers.

In an absolutely innovative way, the issue of civil liability for loss of opportunity is dealt with in the second chapter. In the past years, case-law of the damages arising from medical acts has been characterized by a sort of procedural decisions that emphasized as natural the applicability of this theory in such cases. The author's contribution here, in particular, is innovative and sophisticated.

Following are topics such as post-mortem fertilization and its effects and informed choise, always addressed in the perspective of comparative law.

In my opinion, when Mariana Chaves approaches, in the seventh chapter, the consecration of Autonomy and Dignity of the human being from the Advance Directives, the second step approach is brought and contributes, in a precise way, to something that jurists knew or ought to have know about the issues in medical law. In this environment, dignity and autonomy must go together.

The authors have extensive dogmatic, academic and judicial experience within the themes covered. Thus, they were able to coordinate ideas in a text where all the more stormy themes of the current medical law are dealt with in this work, which makes it necessary and, paradoxically, innovative and already late.

I am therefore of the opinion that such positive arguments shoud be considered as a new point of reflection on the questions of medical law, in which one can not fail to consider that the doctor-patient relationship can not be alienated or captured by law.

In Recife, at 09 days of the month of John.

Larissa Maria de Moraes Leal, PhD

reside dans le devoir d'information, et plus précisément dans l'obrigation pour le médicin de fournir au patient, ou à qui répond de lui, toutes le informations possibles pour que celui-ci puisse exercer son droit, qui repose sur um des príncipes bioéthiques les plus importants: l'autonomie".

Foreword

The field of Bioethics and Medical Law is an inexhaustible source of moral, cultural, juridical, and intellectual challenges.

This new book, by two young but already renowned scholars in the field, Marianna and Eduardo, deals with some of the more visible issues in contemporary Bioethics – visible both for their cultural, even ideological, import, and for their pragmatic relevance, but also for their significance for Law in general.

Bioethics has been pushing the boundaries of Law for more than half a century, and it is to be expected that it will continue to do so – forcing lawyers, as it does philosophers, ethicists and others, to think about problems that are *radically new*, in the sense that they are generated by the intersection of traditional ethical and legal constraints with the ever-expanding possibilities of technological progress[1].

That is not to say that the core of Medical Science, and of Health Care, are changed beyond recognition by that progress, or that they consist mainly of intractable problems and dilemmas, or of tragic choices in resource allocation.

On the contrary, Medicine, and Health Sciences in general, still abide by simple, traditional rules, and that ensures not only the good reputation they enjoy in society at large, but also their prominence in the political and economic debate – a debate which is always unenthusiastic about esoteric topics.

But the fact, nonetheless, is that those intractable problems, dilemmas and tragic choices do exist, and they tend to be superabundant whenever state-of-the-art technology meets the needs, the urgencies, the dramas, even the wild dreams (*v.g.* of human enhancement and immortality), that an informed and eager public multiplies incessantly.

Taking a brief look of those issues that are dealt with in the following chapters, we immediately realize how much the technological possibilities of contemporary Medicine have challenged the traditional ways of thinking about life and death, about procreation, about life before birth, about consent and responsibility, about dignity and vulnerability, about nature, love, genetics, free will, animality, shame, disgust, pride, families, social roles and conventions, about who we are, and what we may become, through the promises and perils of progress – both technological progress and moral progress.

1 Araújo, Fernando (2017), "Desnaturação e Renaturação – O Ciclo da Bioética e o Momento Aristotélico", *Revista Jurídica Luso-Brasileira*, 3/1, 399-412.

No longer can we maintain the innocence of bygone days, that attributed to superhuman powers, or to plain chance, the accidents that characterize human existence, individual health, duties to ourselves, our duties to each other, and our duties to nature. We now tend to believe in the unlimited powers of Medical Science to control, and optimize, the conditions in which we are conceived, we lead an intra-uterine life, we are born, we grow, we love, we procreate, we hurt, we help, we are helped, we suffer and we die – all the while trying to lead a fulfilling and flourishing life within our environment, and under shared social values of liberty, responsibility and empathy.

Fatality has been replaced by human agency – and fatalism has been superseded by issues of politics and justice.

Pushing the boundaries of Law has been, as we said, one of the aims of contemporary Bioethics.

What follows is, then, the analysis of powerful challenges for lawyers; so it should be required reading for all those interested in the fascinating, and sometimes disturbing, paths that Science and Technology, in their interface with human nature, have opened for analysis, reflection and debate *within* Law.

No other field has proven to be more fruitful than Bioethics in adding new topics to Legal doctrine and Legal debates – pushing the boundaries, and then widening the frontiers, of legal thought and practice.

These are some of the issues addressed in the following chapters – always adopting an international perspective, with up-to-date references to the standard literature and the main controversies, although both authors put emphasis on Brazilian and Portuguese Law, the realities they know best.

I'm certain the reader will find this book truly engaging. Read on.

FERNANDO ARAÚJO
Full Professor
Faculdade de Direito da ULisboa

I

Advance Directives and Living Wills – the Role of Patient´s Autonomy In the Brazilian Experience

Eduardo Dantas

Summary: 1. Introduction. **2.** Defining concepts – Or understanding autonomy in end of life situations. **3.** The development of patient´s choice. Ethical and legal aspects. **4.** The Brazilian scenario. The active role of the Federal Council of Medicine. **5.** Conclusions. **6.** References.

> "To violate a person´s autonomy is to treat that person merely as a means, that is, in accordance with others´ goals without regard to that person´s own goals. Such treatment is a fundamental moral violation because autonomous persons are ends in themselves capable of determining their destinies."
>
> Beauchamp and Childress, *Principles of Biomedical Ethics,* 1994, 4th ed., p. 125.

1. Introduction

All over the world, one of the more controversial ethical issues is how to deal with patient´s wishes in a scenario surrounded by the approximation of death. Physicians are trained to postpone death at all costs, but sometimes the patient´s will is to avoid senseless pain when staying alive is not viable anymore (or when life cannot be lived with dignity).

So many questions arise from this conflict: Until when a patient is competent to decide? What are the limits of the patient´s autonomy? What are the limits of medicine, and at what point the thin line of saving a patient´s life and making him suffer for no reason other than keeping him alive is crossed?

And more: in a society where medical issues are brought to the courts in a speed that challenges even common sense, and where the law and statutes can´t keep up to the pace of medical development, what are the limits to what is legal, what is acceptable, what is moral, what is ethical and what is right?

Medicine has evolved in such a speed in the last six decades, that now it is possible to keep a patient artificially alive for years, even against what could be called "the laws of Nature". There are huge debates over the purposes of postponing death at all costs, even if means leaving the patient alive and suffering in a vegetative state, just to satisfy the family´s wishes. For some, this is a natural response (and obligation) of medicine. To others, it is just playing God beyond the limits of science.

There is no easy answer to these issues, but a consistent solution is under construction in different parts of the world, leading towards the respect of the patient´s will, and recognizing the importance of obtaining the patient´s consent, whenever it is possible, respecting autonomy and choice.

2. Defining concepts – Or understanding autonomy in end of life situations

Informed consent is the authorization given by the patient to undergo treatment, based on the knowledge of the nature of a medical procedure, and be submitted to risks, side effects, possible complications, benefits and alternatives to the proposed treatment. In other words, it is the acceptance of the services to be delivered by a healthcare professional, after understanding what is being consented to.

We're a long way from the days when physicians told patients what they needed and patients agreed without question. Although some patients still have an "I'll do whatever you say, doctor" attitude, they're in the minority. In today's world, different people react to proposed treatments or tests differently, often as a result of their varied backgrounds, financial status, values, attitudes and perspectives.

The paradox of contemporary medicine is that a constant expansion of therapeutic options makes decoding these options increasingly difficult. In legal terms, this new situation has been transposed into a growing demand for patient participation in decision-making which seems to express the notion that anxiety caused by being subjected to some kind of medical dictatorship creates the need to even out a relationship which is by essence asymmetrical. To this recent culture is added a growing trend to judiciarisation[1] which challenges medicine to respond to contradictory imperatives: give the best possible care, but within mandatory limits and constraints, or confronted with hostility.

When it comes to end of life situation, another piece of human drama is added: the patient – as a corollary of the principle of respect for human dignitiy, has the right to be informed about his situation, the prognosis and the possible or expected outcome, and then be an active player in the decision-making process.

In other words: in a terminal situation, the patient has the right to refuse treatment, if there is no possibility of staying alive without suffering or a minimum standard of quality, and can opt to receive just palliative care, leaving life to follow its natural course, without artificially postponing death.

One of the biggest problems in accepting this decision is that some segments of society still thinks that refusing treatment is the same as authorizing euthanasia.

Euthanasia is the act of provoking, or facilitate the death of another person who is suffering from a serious and, for the most part, painful illness. It depends on a clear act, such as the application of high doses of sedating, or lethal substances in a terminal patient. It differs from the assisted suicide because in the latter, the help to die is explicitly requested by a patient who is no longer able to move, or to act on their own in this regard.

The orthotanasia, is the suspension, reduction or withdrawal of medication, equipment, or procedures that serve to artificially prolong the life of a patient, abbreviating his suffering, and allowing life follow its natural path to extinction. Not resuscitating one patient who is suffering a cardiorespiratory arrest seems to be a good example of it.

In diverse path follows the dysthanasia, which is prolonging life of a patient without any viable prospect of cure or improvement by artificial means.

The treatment of terminally ill patients, and the postponing of end of life issues, has always been one of the greatest dilemmas faced

1 On this topic, DEMICHEL's "*Au nom de quoi? Libre propos d'une juriste sur la médicalisation de la vie*".

by doctors, who were trained and taught to face death as a defeat, and the prolongation of life as the only acceptable procedure.

Just recently, the issue has become subject of legislation in different countries, strenghtening the idea that the patients needed to play a major role, regulating thus how autonomy could be exercised, in order to bring legal safety to the decisions, pushing liability and criminal responsibility away from the doctor-patient relationship.

3. The development of patient´s choice. Ethical and legal aspects

Refusing treatment is always an event situated at the centre of a profusion of concerns. The need for recognition is probably one of the most significant of them. This need for recognition that Paul Ricoeur[2] analyzed with great precision exists in both patient and doctor.

Patients want doctors to recognize their individuality and their complexity. Refusal can be an expression of this need and a request for euthanasia is frequently a call for help rather than evidence of any real desire to end life.

But doctors also need recognition from patients, not so much in the form of gratitude, but in terms of recognition for their competence, their sense of responsibility and the legitimacy and specificity of the values which the medical profession upholds.

To these two components could probably be added the expression of a need for social recognition, recognition of a need expressed by a public call for help from both protagonists in the act of caring. One specific characteristic of caring is the statement of an act of solidarity so that the "private" dialogue between patient and physician is frequently part of a quest for social harmony. When these demands are claimed by both parties, it is easy to understand that the two (or three) recognitions may not coincide. This may be the case when a sick person entertains iron-bound convictions that do not allow him to take account of the concern for professional – not to mention legal – responsibilities that inhabits the doctor. Or a doctor who is excessively infatuated with some therapeutic project and resents criticism from the patient.

2 P. Ricoeur, Parcours de la reconnaissance, Paris, Stock, 2004

Or it could be also recognition that medicine is a culture that finds it unacceptable that traditional beliefs which they consider to be irrational be allowed to challenge their modern practices backed by scientific evidence. As can be seen from all these examples, solving the issues on a pragmatic case by case basis is not the way to developing guidelines.

One answer lies in the fact that the way many of us can expect to live, age and die has changed dramatically over the past quarter of a century. In many countries, advances in basic living conditions, healthcare and medical technology mean that *most* of us are living to a good age, and that *many* of us are living to a very good age in spite of the illnesses or fragility which ordinarily beset us. When in the past we had good reasons to fear an *early* death, today many of us fear living *too long*, and we fear that medical interventions will unreasonably prolong our dying as well. When in the past we had good reasons to fear a painful and uncomfortable *aging* and *dying*, today with advances in the management of chronic illnesses and palliative medicine, we are more likely to be fearful of *living* not with pain and discomfort, but instead with the perceived degradation of physical dependence or mental incompetence.

Boundaries of this subject are yet to be discovered. In *Old Law, New Medicine*[3], Sheila McLean points out:

> "The fundamental taboos which surround the very subject of death permits the perpetuation of an approach to it which may have a number of consequences. First, those who actively choose death may be regarded as irrational or lacking in legal competence. This is particularly so when medicine can offer hope of a cure or palliation of symptoms.
> ...
> Second, some individuals may be so afraid of a life without prolonged quality that they choose suicide as an option. Angell, for example, has noted that: 'The very high suicide rate in older Americans is due partly to concern that they will be unable to stop treatment if hospitalized... Some people now fear living more than dying, because they dread becoming prisoners of technology.'

3 (1999), London, Pandora, p. 140-141.

> ...
> Finally, medical advances require resolution of the question of what is to be done in respect of the person who is incompetent, with no hope of recovery and with no clear advance expression of wishes. Strict adherence to the principle of the sanctity of life results in such individuals being maintained in an insentient form for what, in some cases, may be a very long time. Without clear justifications for the termination of treatment, life which has no quality for the person living it will be prolonged merely because the technology to do so exists."

The discussion about patient´s autonomy is neither new nor original.[4] But it is interesting to see that all movements made, both in the legal and ethical fields, lead towards the same conclusion. Different jurisdictions, with completely unrelated legal backgrounds, are finding the same solutions.

Historically, the ability to force treatment on unwilling patients derived from a need-for-treatment justification. This approach started to change in the 1960s, mostly in the United States, when there was a gradual move toward the "dangerous patient" justification—unwanted treatment could be imposed only if or when the patient presented a significant risk of harming himself or others. Under this new system, patient advocates began to press for the patient's right to determine what was done to his own body, creating instances in which the committed patient could decline treatment with medication. As these matters began to make legal appearances in the U.S. countrywide, virtually every involved court recognized some substantial patient interest in a right to refuse treatment.[5]

---

4 Regarding the historical background on this issue, I refer to my paper entitled "When consent is not enough: the construction and development of the modern concept of autonomy", published by Lex Medicinae (Portugal, vol. 15, 2011, p. 101-112).

5 In the same sense, see *Vacco v. Quill,* 117 S.Ct. 2293 (1997) or *Washington v. Glucksberg,* 117 S.Ct. 2258 (1997).

In 1989, deciding a case in the British courts[6], Lord Donaldson MR stated in his ruling that:

> "The ability of the ordinary adult to exercise a free choice in deciding whether to accept or refuse medical treatment and to choose between treatments is not to be dismissed as desirable but inessential. It is a crucial factor in relation to all medical treatment".

In 1997, Article 5 of the Oviedo Convention (European Convention of Human Rights and Biomedicine), clearly stated:

> "An intervention in the health field may only be carried out after the person concerned has given free and informed consent. This person shall beforehand be given appropriate information as to the purpose and nature of the intervention as well as on its consequence and risks. The person concerned may freely withdraw at any time."

Very similar to that, and just a few years later, UNESCO´s Universal Declaration on Biomedicine and Human Rights (2005) recognized the same principle of respect for autonomy, also in its article 5:

> "The autonomy of persons to make decisions, while taking responsibility for those decisions and respecting the autonomy of others, is to be respected".

In 1994, the United States Congress acknowledged patients' overall rights to refuse medical treatment in certain circumstances, even if such refusal would result in death, enacting the Patient Self Determination Act[7]. (the "Act") in an effort to encourage patients to exercise their common law rights to refuse treatment. The Act applies to licensed health care facilities which receive Medicare or Medicaid program funds. The Act requires hospitals, nursing homes and hospices

---

6 *In Re F (Mental Patient: Sterilisation) (1990) 2 AC 1.*

7 (a.k.a. the "Danforth Act") See 42 U.S.C. §1395cc (1994).

to furnish certain information to the patient/resident at the time of admission. This written information concerns an individual's rights under State law and the written policies of the provider regarding implementation of the patient's advance directives. The facility must also document in the individual's medical record whether the individual has an advance medical directive. The provision of an individual's care may not be conditioned upon execution of an advance directive.

In France, patient´s right to advance directive and to appoint a person to act as proxy (not necessarily a relative, but someone who will be entrusted on enforcing the patient´s will in case of unconsciousness, or inability to speak for itself) is regulated by the law of March 4th, 2004 (commonly known as *Loi Kouchner*).

Recently, Portugal enacted the Law 25/2012, which regulates advance directives, living wills, health care proxy and creates a National Registry of Advance Directives.

All of this combined represents a quick but comprehensive view on the complexity of the situation, and how seriously the debate over autonomy and the patient´s right to decide his own fate when facing a terminal disease is.

In the precise words of Kristinsson[8],

> "Personal deliberation might be valued for its ability to bring out, express, and create the distinct point of view of the individual in question, and for making it possible for the individual to steer the course of her life according to that distinct point of view. An individual´s "point of view" is a complex, dynamic outcome of emotions, judgments, beliefs, desires, habits, and character, and all of these are in turn affected by upbringing and other contingent circumstances".

From all this comparative background, it seems that there is no doubt that we are heading towards the recognition of the patient´s right to exercise autonomy, not only during treatment, but also deciding when it should finish.

---

8 KRISTINSSON, Sigurdur. Autonomy and informed consent: A mistaken Association?, *Medicine, Health Care and Philosophy*. DOI 10.1007/s11019-007-9048-4, Springer, 2007.

4. The Brazilian scenario. The active role of the Federal Council of Medicine

The Brazilian situation regarding advance directives is very peculiar. While other countries have been long discussing the subject, either in court or through legislation, the issue has been solemnly ignored by politicians, leaving a void in legislation, and thus creating insecurity for the health care professionals.

There is no provision in Brazilian law, regulation or establishing guidelines for the use (and even validity) of advance directives in a terminal situation. Physicians have to rely on the interpretation of various codes and legal norms, in an exercise of legal interpretation they are not used (or trained) to.

According to the Federal Constitution, a patient has the right to refuse medical treatment, based on the article 5, section II, which states that nobody can be forced to do, or be compelled not to do something against his or her will, unless determined by law.

In the same sense, medical treatment can be refused in respect for the patients philosophical convictions and religious beliefs, according to sections VI and VIII of the same article, which guarantees such freedom. In other words, it's a constitutional right that the patient's will must prevail over the therapeutic option chosen by the doctor, even if technical and professional arguments are ignored. Being a conscious decision, taken by a competent patient, after proper information, it must be respected.

References of the patient's right to refuse treatment are scattered all over Brazilian legislation, without a specific legal act. The Civil Code states, in its article 15, that "*no one can be constrained to submit, with risk to life, to a medical treatment or surgical intervention*".

The terms of the article are imprecise, because the expression "with risk to life" may lead to the false conclusion that, if there's no risk of dying, the patient could be constrained, or forced, to accept treatment or surgical intervention, which is not the spirit of the law.

The new Civil Code, enacted in 2002, presents a twist in medical responsibility, changing what was considered the main physician's obligation – saving human lives no matter what – and giving powers (and responsibilities, as a consequence) to patients and legal surrogates, letting them interfere and decide their own fate, according to the bioethical principles of autonomy.

In the same spirit of law, the Elder's Statute (Estatuto do Idoso) guarantees, in article 17, to people of more than 65 years of age, which are sound mind and sane, the right to choose what they consider the most favorable health treatment.

The aforementioned Statute does not make any reference to risk of death as a condition to carry out the right to choose a therapeutic option. The only possibility of restraint for the patient is to be insane and lacking of his mental integrity, regardless of his clinical condition. In this situation, the doctor can only proceed his own personal option of treatment if a) the patient cannot express his will; b) the relatives or legal surrogates cannot be found; and c) there's immediate and real risk of death.

Another expression of the patient's autonomy in the Brazilian legal system is contained in the article 10 of the Statute of Organ Donations and Transplants), which favours, in its paragraph, the patient's consent in any situation, in spite of the doctor's decision, demanding the express consent of the receiver, after counseling about the risks of the transplant procedure. That means that, even in real and immediate risk of death, the patient can decide to submit or not to the risks of transplantation.

The same reasoning, though, can be applied to radical surgical procedures, administration of medicine, chemotherapy and blood transfusion, considered to many as form of "transplantation"

It is perhaps worth mentioning, at this point, a law enforced by the State of São Paulo[9], which guarantees to the State's health service users the right to receive clear and adequate information on therapies and therapeutic procedures, in respect for ethical and cultural values.

Two other States – Paraná and Minas Gerais – also passed laws for public health services users' protection[10], stressing patient's autonomy as a principle to be observed and enforced.

It's clear, then, that these modern pieces of legislation take into consideration the patient's will, in spite of his clinical state and condition, presenting legal mechanisms to enforce his right of choice,

9 State Law n. 10.241/1999 – São Paulo

10 State Law n. 14.254/2003 – Paraná and State Law n. 16.279/2006 – Minas Gerais

rejecting medical or judicial impositions, respecting the principles of dignity of the human being.

Another conclusion that can be reached is that the bioethical principle of Beneficence must be interpreted under the patient's view, since he is the addressee of medical intervention, and even if the Medical Ethics Code guarantees the physician (article 22) discretionary action in a life and death situation, this discretion cannot oppose constitutional rights.

There are, though, winds of change, provided not by legislators, but by physicians themselves. By August 2012, the Federal Council of Medicine approved a new resolution (CFM n. 1995/2012) allowing doctors to withhold procedures or withdraw treatments designed to keep a terminal patient alive, provided the patient or his legal surrogate expresses the wish to do so.

> RESOLUTION CFM 1.995/2012 (August 31st, 2012)
> Article 1 – Defining advanced directives as a set of wishes, previously and expressely manifested by the patient, about the health care or treatments he/she wants – or not – to receive in the moment he/she loses the ability to express, freely and autonomously, his/her will.
> Article 2 – When deciding about health care or treatment of patients who are incapable of communicating, or to express freely and independently their will, the physician shall take into consideration their advanced directives.
> Section 1 – If the patient has designated a proxy for that purpose, the proxy´s informations should be taken into consideration by the physician.
> Section 2 – The physician shall disregard the patient´s advanced directives or proxy´s informations when they are, after his analysis, conflicting with the principles established by the Medical Ethics Code.
> Section 3 – The advance directives shall prevail against any medical opinion and against the patient´s family wishes.
> Section 4 – The physician will register, on the patient´s chart, the advanced directives that are directly communicated to him by the patient.
> Section 5 – If no advanced directives are established, nor a proxy has been designated, and if there is no family members

> available to decide, or if they have conflicting requests, the physician – when found necessary and convenient – shall submit the case to the hospital´s Ethics Committee. If there´s no such committee, the case must be submitted to the Regional and Federal Council of Medicine, to provide solid grounds in order to solve ethical conflicts.
> Article 3 – This Resolution shall enter into force on the date of its publication.

Such a Resolution is not an statute, but rather than just being an ethical guideline, and facing the lack of regulation on the matter, it assumes capital importance and (at least temporarily) fulfills the legal gap, since the Federal Council of Medicine was created by a Federal Law, and among the competencies that were given to it, there is the power to enact guidelines that will oblige physicians during the exercise of the medical profession.

It's an important step towards giving the patient the possibility of regaining control over his own life, allowing him to die with dignity. The main result of this Resolution is to recognize that dying with dignity is a part of a greater scenario, which is living with dignity.

Although it may seem justifiable to state that patients may wish to be and remain at all times in complete control over matters regarding their personal health, this simple statement of principle bears little relationship to reality. People who are confronted with pain, disease, approaching death, are bound to feel diminished by the awareness of their own weakness and therefore lose some of their autonomy to the extent that they no longer know what it is they want or can accept and are not even able to express themselves.

By their side, or more often than not, facing them, are physicians or carers whose strength is reinforced by their own science, despite some doubts and hesitation at times, and who wish to accomplish their mission which is to apply in full treatment which they consider to be the most appropriate in the circumstances to alleviate, cure, or delay the advent of death.

But what is left of patient autonomy, of the notion of consent that the patient is requested to give and of the need to create conditions in which freedom of consent – which everyone agrees must be "informed" – can be exercised? Can there be consent if, as we have seen, there is no possibility of refusal?

This was the question that the Brazilian Code of Medical Ethics (another Resolution from the Federal Council of Medicine) dated 2009 attempted to answer, so as to provide patients with more autonomy of decision as regards medical care and ensure more equality in the relationship between doctors and patients.

The Code enshrines the notion that patient consent must prevail and in other words states that, in the light of information and advice supplied by healthcare providers and in consultation with them, patients are entitled to take decisions regarding their own health. Doctors must respect wishes expressed by patients after informing them of the consequences of their decisions.

When refusing to undergo or continue treatment represents a threat to life, physicians must do their utmost to convince patients that they should accept essential treatment. No medical act nor any treatment may be applied without securing free and informed consent from the person concerned. There is, though, a legal gap in here, since consent may be withdrawn at any time, but the criminal code forbids physicians to interrupt life-saving treatments. This inconsistency has yet to be faced by Court, since no claim has posed this issue up to now.

These, are, therefore, the ethical foundations of patient autonomy and right to refuse treatment, in Brazil, inserted in the Code of Medical Ethics:

> Art. 41-[The doctor shall not] Shorten the patient's life, albeit at its request or at its legal representative.
> Sole paragraph – In cases of incurable and terminal disease, the doctor must provide all palliative care available without undertaking unnecessary diagnostic, therapeutic or obstinate actions, always taking into consideration the wishes expressed by the patient or, in his impossibility, of his legal representative ".

Amongst the Fundamental Principles of Medicine, elected by the Medical Ethics Code, the one described in section XXII says verbatim that "in terminal and irreversible clinical situations, physicians avoid carrying out unnecessary diagnostic and therapeutic procedures and allow the patients under his care all appropriate palliative care. "

The aforementioned resolution is grounded in the claim of the defense of constitutional principles such as human dignity, and the prohibition of inhuman or degrading treatment, clearly stated in Articles 1°, III and 5º, III – of the Federal Constitution. These principles are effectively important, that add up to the bioethical principle of autonomy, but they conflict with the protection of life (the sanctity of life, as found in the foreign doctrine).

When dealing with the existence and recognition of a patient's right to die with dignity and autonomy, Leticia Ludwig Möller shows well the conflict faced between the ethically desirable and legally permissible:[11]

> "The excessive and inappropriate use of technologies applied to the medical treatment of patients in the terminal stage, leading to the prolongation of a painful end of life (often beyond what would be desired by the patient himself, disregarding his right to exercise autonomy, conforming the idea and the need to affirm the existence of a right to die with dignity. The expression "right to die" or "right to a dignified death" can now be found in studies about end of life seeking the dialogue between different areas of knowledge, such as medicine, ethics and law. The advocates of the right to die with dignity, in general, are glimpsing the patient's terminal condition that is exposed to treatments that merely extend the time of his death, bringing him no benefits, but only pain and suffering – not often wishing these authors extend this defense to the practice of euthanasia (active). Dying with dignity so often relate to the idea of dying in peace, with physical and spiritual integrity, or even, to die at the right time, with comfort and relief from suffering.
> (...)
> We share the understanding of Ronald Dworkin, that the way we die has importance, and in general, the right of the individual to his death is a reflex of how he lived must be respected, that this time keep a consistency with the values and beliefs expressed in life – especially if this is the manifest desire of the ailing, and within the limits (as stated above)."

11 In Right to die with dignity and autonomy. Ed (Publisher). Juruá, Curitiba, 2007. pages 95-98.

Another important aspect to be considered is the fact that the practice of palliative medicine is now a reality in the vast majority of hospitals in Brazil, being positive in order not to deprive the conviviality of terminally ill patient from their families. This stance, according to its advocates, meets one of the pillars of bioethics, which is the principle of autonomy, the patient's right to decide the course of their own treatment. It would still be consistent with respect for human dignity, the principle developed in the first article of our Federal Constitution.

Examining the Medical Ethics Code, Leo Pessini adds:[12]

> "(...) we noticed significant change of emphasis. The goal of medicine is not only maximizing the lifetime of a person. The aim of medical attention is the health of the human being and the criterion to evaluate their procedures is whether they will benefit the patient or not (cf. art. 2nd). The commitment to health, especially if understood as global welfare of the person and not just the absence of disease, it opens up the possibility for other issues in the treatment of the terminally ill, and the healing issues. Even so, it remains a steadfast conviction, also found in earlier codes, that "The doctor must keep absolute respect for human life (...)" (art. 6). This tension between benefiting the patient with palliative treatments, which may shorten his life but promote his physical and mental well-being, and the absolutism of the value of human life in its biological sense, produces a dilemma that some doctors prefer to settle in favour of prolonging life."

From a strictly rational point of view, death is just one of many aspects of life. Nothing more natural. However, talking about death, this companion that is increasingly present from the moment we are born, it causes us discomfort such that we turned it into a real taboo. We associate it with fear, frustration, pain, suffering and despair. Trying to ignore the undeniable reality of its existence, we avoid talking about it: we deny children the understanding of the phenomenon of death

12 In his article "Dysthanasia: some reflections from the bioethical Brazilian reality", published in the journal Bioethics 2004, Vol. 12, No. 01.

and the right to bid farewell to the beloved ones; we deny ourselves share the grief with loved ones; we deny health professions students a deep discussion on the topic that would help them to better deal with the matter within their professional practice. We created an illusion of immortality, thus wasting the opportunity that the acceptance of our finitude gives us: the opportunity to reflect on life and the perception that the time we have is limited, and therefore precious. Live it with quality is the true translation of what it is a life well lived.

It is within this perspective of emphasis to a life of dignity and quality that the healthcare professionals who are dedicated to palliative care work. Such care seek to relieve the suffering of patients whose medical diagnostics indicate that they have no chance of healing, through symptom control (not only physical, but in different orders) and the promotion of a lifetime with the best possible quality until the last moment. It is the quest for "good death".

Inherent to palliative care is the attempt to rescue an experience more human in the relationship between the patient and the professional staff that takes care of him. Special attention is also given to the humanization of the processes of death and mourning, in prolonged illnesses that are usually intense and characterized by long periods of emotional burnout and stress.

In palliative care, the person is treated, not the disease. This seemingly simple change makes a big difference. It opens space for a perception of singularities of the individual, thus leading to a more accurate understanding of their real needs. Treating the patient with respect and preserving his dignity is only possible when it is considered in its context and its nuances. It is a sine qua non condition so we can see him in his condition of human being, rather than sick, that we are open to listen to their concerns, fears, desires and feelings, whether they manifest in verbal or unsaid.

Kübler-Ross points out five stages of dying, each with its own characteristics. At the denial stage, the patient uses this defense mechanism in an attempt to cope with the anxiety facing his own the death. At the stage of anger, arises a revolt against the diagnosis, the prognosis, and often against God and against those who are around him. The patient may show up aggressive toward his family members and the professionals who take care of him. At the bargaining stage, there is an attempt to negotiate his healing, doing good deeds to be rewarded for them. The fourth stage described by the author is depression, in which the patient comes into contact with a profound sense of loss and may prove to be silent and isolated from others. Finally, there is the stage of acceptance, in which the despair gives place to a feeling of peace. It is important to stress that, although these stages serve as parameters for the understanding of the process by which the patient passes, they do not present themselves in a rigid order and the way they are experienced, as well as the duration of each, is variable for each individual. It is important to respect each of these phases allowing the patient to experience them.[13]

While in traditional medicine the health professional seem encouraged to turn to attempt to extend the duration of life avoiding death, medicine that attempts to palliative care is seeking to prolong what makes us human, preserving the maximum freedom of making conscious choices. Life is not only considered in its biological sense, but also includes social, psychological and relational aspects. While there is life there is also the potential for emotional growth, intra and interpersonal.

Implied to a discussion about palliative care is the issue of how human beings are perceived, because the vision of man that the healthcare professional has, directly affects his attitude and his work – whether he is aware of his ideas or not.

If the ideas of the professionals are inserted within a paradigm that assigns to the man an essence of identity, he will not be seen as amenable to changes and growth, but as someone always equal to himself, thus not affected by the other. From this perspective there is an appreciation of stability: the human conflicts are viewed negatively, taken as imbalances that must be banned for threatening stability. This man is thought of as a passive being, and therefore being incumbent to the health professional the keeping of knowledge and total responsibility for the course of his treatment.

There is, however, another paradigm that has been strengthening and which provides the basis for the changes requested by the palliative medicine: the man seen as procedural being, i.e. a man thata builds himself, actively, as he lives. This means that he never remains static

13 KÜBLER-ROSS, E. On death and dying: what patients have to teach doctors, nurses, religious and their own relatives. Ed (Publisher). Martins Fontes Sao Paulo, 1996.

or reaches the end of constructing himself. On the contrary, it lies in a continuous becoming, overtaking what is from what is about to becoming. The processuality of man takes place through the meeting with the other, in a dialectical relationship in which affects and is also affected, being the mutual affectation the requirement for growth. The conflicts, far from being seen as negative, are the promoters of growth and they stimulate and develop the potential of adaptation.

The emphasis, in this paradigmatic vision, is in the potential of human beings to make changes, to reframe their experiences and establish life projects for themselves. His ability to make conscious choices gives the possibility to seek self-fulfilment creatively and responsibly. Within this perspective, the patient is not passive towards health professionals and diagnoses received.

The paradigm that sees the patient as a whole human being, this has autonomy over his lifetime. So there is no space for a health professional who presents himself authoritatively: possible interventions and the implications of each of them must necessarily be discussed with clarity and directness between doctor, team, patient and family. With this, the dignity of the patient is mantained and he is allowed to make choices that, in his concern, are the most appropriate, i.e. meeting his best interests. When talking about choices, we do not mean only those that involve the balancing of risks and benefits of possible treatments and medical interventions, but rather we include the resolutions of life and farewells.

To deny the patient the clarification on his actual conditions is not a way to protect him. Rather, it means leaving him alone without the chance to share his woes and feeling himself betrayed by realizing that he cannot fully rely on those whose care he is submitted to. When the family decides to keep secrets or lie to the patient about his diagnosis and prognosis, it will create an emotional barrier that will hamper the free expression of affections in relationships.

Being able to go through the end of life consciously and feeling himself valued and respected enriches the life of the patient in order to promote a greater sense of emotional strengthening. This is an important prerequisite for the establishment of clearer priorities and for a deeper connection with the loved ones.

Palliative care also fulfill the role of helping the relatives of the patient to face the process of coming across the pain of the situation impending loss of a beloved (family) member.

The familiar universe is systemic, and therefore the impact of the existence of a member in need of palliative care is impacting to each of the other members and to the family unit as a whole. The family faces a long and anticipatory mourning, since the feeling of loss is settled from the diagnosis, and the emotional issues that arise during this period of stress need to be recognized and addressed.

Being able to express the pain and share feelings promotes individual and family strengthening. Depart from the patient does not relieve pain from anyone and causes to the patient the extra pain of abandonment in life.

To be empowered to act appropriately in palliative care, a health care professional needs some training which goes beyond the technical field. As important as the safety in knowledge acquired is personal preparation which allows coming across his own limitations and with the confrontation of doubts and anguish that the theme of death rises, and yet what we call interpersonal preparation, indispensable when the proposal is truly monitoring the patient, taking him and his family in his afflictions and acting as facilitator of the relationship between both of them, in favor of a dignified life.

The great virtue of this resolution was to bring onto the stage the debate which hitherto remained confined to the corridors of hospitals. Science has evolved to the point of allowing to prolong artificially a terminal life indefinitely, under suffering, mechanically, without purpose and at any cost, medicine is avoiding its primary objective. At this point, absolutely defendable to the debate of the topic, even for that criticism launched allow its improvement, both directly and without pretense.

5. Conclusions

It is important to recognize, however, that some people who express support for a 'right to die,' only do so in a highly qualified way. Many people who think that medicine often sustains or prolongs life unreasonably, and who feel helpless to oppose its momentum, often assert a 'right to die' when what they are really claiming is the 'right to refuse burdensome or futile treatment'. They are not interested in asserting *complete* control *over death*, but seek instead, to reclaim *some* control over the *manner of their dying.*

There is, of course, a clear and established ethical tradition describing the legitimate scope and limit of choice with respect to the circumstances and timing of death. Mindful of the dignity and consequent inviolability of human life, the Catholic ethical tradition stands with traditional Western medical ethics, in recognizing that the direct and voluntary killing of an innocent human person, at every stage and in every state of life, is always gravely wrong.[14] When life-saving or life-sustaining treatment is withdrawn or withheld with the intention of ending a person's life, this is an unethical action or omission, irrespective of any good motive, and morally equivalent to euthanasia or suicide.[15]

Yet this tradition also recognizes that, sometimes, respecting human dignity and caring for patients can require the avoidance of over-treatment as well as under-treatment. Within the life of every human person there are limits to the extent to which life and health should or can be actively pursued. While there will often be good reasons to do things which protect or prolong life, there may concurrently be good reasons *not* to do so, such as great risks or burdens of various kinds for the person whose life would be prolonged or for those who would be engaged in her care.

Therefore, Catholic medical ethics describes treatments which have become, or are likely to be, *futile* or *overly-burdensome* as 'extraordinary', 'heroic' or 'disproportionate'. To forego such treatments is not the equivalent of euthanasia or suicide, but an acceptance of the human condition in the face of death.[16] This is not a choice for death, but a choice about how to live while dying.

Provided that the 'right to refuse treatment' does not embrace any right to refuse treatment *precisely* so that death will occur sooner, this right is substantially different from any alleged right to become or to be made dead, by whatever means. What we are to make of this latter right – whether or not there is a specific 'natural' or 'basic human' right to have one's life intentionally shortened through suicide, assisted suicide or voluntary euthanasia – in asking 'is there a right to die?'

14 John Paul II. *Evangelium Vitae: Encyclical Letter on The Value and Inviolability of Human Life*. Homebush: St Pauls, 1995, n. 57.

15 EV n. 65

16 *ibid*

It is the central thesis of the common law doctrine of trespass to the person that the voluntary choices and decisions of an adult person of sound mind concerning what is or is not done to his or her body must be respected and accepted, irrespective of what others, including doctors, may think is in the interests of that particular person. To this general thesis there is an exception: a person cannot consent to the infliction of grievous bodily harm without 'good reason'. But save in this exceptional case, the common law respects and preserves the autonomy of adult persons of sound mind with respect to their bodies. By doing so, the common law accepts that a person has rights of control and self-determination in respect of her or his body that other persons must respect. Those rights can only be altered with the consent of the person concerned. Thus the legal requirement of consent to bodily interference protects the autonomy and dignity of the individual and limits the power of others to interfere with that person's body.

Although the law's respect for the unique dignity of every person is the same, the protection of the physical integrity which is required to preserve the dignity of one person may change from time to time and it may differ from the protection of physical integrity required to preserve the dignity of another. Differing measures of protection are required according to the physical and mental capabilities of individuals at particular times; the baby whose dignity is respected by being carried and cared for by his or her parents grows into a man or woman whose dignity would be offended by such treatment; a donation of blood by a person of full age and understanding may enhance dignity, while the extraction of blood from a person who is incapable of consenting is an invasion of that person's physical integrity. Human dignity requires the whole personality to be respected: the right to physical integrity is a condition of human dignity but the gravity of any invasion of physical integrity depends on its effect not only on the body but also on the mind and on the self-perception.

Refusal of treatment is never simply a confrontation, be it rebellion against what is perceived as the medical "order", or a claim for absolute freedom of choice or a misapprehension of the true situation. In the wings, there is always a misunderstanding, something left unsaid, on the part of the doctor, the family, or a person who may, or may not, be ailing. But perhaps it is in just such situations that the medical profession must show the true colours of its ethics.

6. References

BEAUCHAMP, Tom L., CHILDRESS, J. Principles of biomedical ethics. New York, Oxford University Press, 1979.

DANTAS, Eduardo. Direito Médico. Rio de Janeiro, Editora GZ, 2009.

DANTAS, Eduardo. *When consent is not enough: the construction and development of the modern concept of autonomy*. In Lex Medicinae – Revista Portuguesa de Direito da Saúde. Year 8, n. 15, Coimbra, Coimbra Editora, 2011, p. 101-112.

DANTAS, Eduardo. *How informed should consent be? A brief analysis on consent and autonomy under the European Convention on Human Rights and Biomedicine.* In Lex Medicinae – Revista Portuguesa de Direito da Saúde. Year 9, n. 17, Coimbra, Coimbra Editora, 2012, p. 51-64.

DEMICHEL, F.. Au nom de quoi? Libre propos d'une juriste sur la médicalisation de la vie. Bordeaux, Les Études Hospitalières, 2006.

Federal Council of Medicine – Brazil. Resolution 1.931 (2009) [Medical Ethics Code]

Federal Council of Medicine – Brazil. Resolution 1.995 (2012)

HOWARTH, L., Autonomy, A Study in Philosophical Psychology and Ethics. New Haven, Yale University Press, 1986.

John Paul II. *Evangelium Vitae: Encyclical Letter on The Value and Inviolability of Human Life*. Homebush: St Pauls, 1995.

KRISTINSSON, Sigurdur. Autonomy and informed consent: A mistaken Association? *Medicine, Health Care and Philosophy*. DOI 10.1007/s11019-007-9048-4, Springer, 2007.

KÜBLER-ROSS, E. Sobre a morte e o morrer: o que os doentes têm para ensinar a médicos, enfermeiras, religiosos e aos seus próprios parentes. Martins Fontes, São Paulo, 1996.

McLEAN, Sheila. Old Law, New Medicine. London, Pandora, 1999.

MöLLER , Leticia Ludwig. Direito à morte com dignidade e autonomia. Juruá, Curitiba, 2007.

PESSINI, Leo. "Distanásia: algumas reflexões bioéticas a partir da realidade brasileira ", in Revista Bioética, CFM, Brasília, 2004, Vol. 12, n. 01.

RICOEUR, Paul. Parcours de la reconnaissance. Paris, Stock, 2004.

II

THE INAPPLICABILITY OF THE LOSS OF A CHANCE THEORY IN CASES OF MEDICAL RESPONSIBILITY IN THE BRAZILIAN LEGAL SYSTEM

Eduardo Dantas

Abstract: With the growth of legal demands related to medical practice in the last ten years, Loss of a Chance Theory rapidly found acceptance in Brazilian courtrooms, being used as ground for granting reparation regarding civil liability. This brief study aims to discuss the inadequacy of adopting this theory without further thinking or adaptation, since the current legal background in Brazil points out to stress the actual damage, not the presumed one, especially on an environment surrounded by unpredictability and random outcomes as the medical sciences.

Keywords: Loss of a chance. Comparative Law. Brazilian Legal System.

Summary: **1.** Introduction **2.** The Brazilian Legal System regarding compensation and torts **3.** The inadequacy of the loss of a chance theory in medical activity **4.** An analysis on recent jurisprudential developments. **5.** Conclusions. **6.** References.

1. INTRODUCTION

No one denies the importance of using comparative law as a means to bring new light to old problems, and as a valid way of proposing solutions to new challenges in a country´s legal system. But that can not be achieved without proper adaptation.

In general lines that´s what´s currently happening with the theory of Loss of a Chance. Developed in France and Italy, and embraced in England, United States and Spain, this theory has been recently adopted in Brazilian courtrooms, without appropriate discussions on the validity of the application of its doctrine in Brazilian Law.

The loss of a chance concept was originally discussed during a trial in the French *Cour de Cassation*, back in 1965, reviewing a case of medical responsibility, where the physician was considered guilty, because of a wrong diagnosis that prevented the patient from achieving a cure.[1]

Perhaps one of the most famous cases in French legal history, regarding the loss of a possibility in medical treatment was the Affair Perruche. In 1982, a pregnant Josette Perruche discovered symptoms of what proved to be rubella on her four-year-old daughter. She told her physician that, if she too were infected, she would have an abortion rather than run the risk of giving birth to a severely handicapped child. Her physician arranged for two blood tests with a local lab and after reading the results informed Josette that she was in fact immunized against rubella. Both physician and lab were, in varying ways, quite wrong. About a year after his birth, Nicolas Perruche began manifesting major neurological deficits: deafness, partial blindness, and severe brain damage. For their part, his parents, Josette and Christian, initiated legal action against both the physician and the testing lab that had misdiagnosed Josette's condition and effectively nullified her right to an abortion.

The question was just what could they claim damages for under the terms of the 1974 law legalizing abortion? Courts were prepared to indemnify women in Josette's position for their loss of choice. But Josette and Christian Perruche went further, first seeking compensation to themselves for the medical liabilities Nicolas had suffered, and later acting for Nicolas himself in a separate suit and seeking direct compensation to their child, rather than to themselves. In choosing that course, however, they encountered a formidable juridical obstacle: the principle of "respect for the dignity of the human person."

Perruches' cause was greatly boosted in the mid-1980s when decisions of the Council of State and the Court of Cassation established the theoretical possibility of distinguishing between a child's life, which clearly could not be indemnified, and a child's handicaps, which could be. At that point, the case entered a new level of disputation.

The defendants had already conceded their liability to both Josette and Christian. But to extend that liability to Nicolas, they argued, was to stretch it beyond all reason. His deficits, after all, did

---

1 According to BIONDI, in Teoria da perda de uma chance na responsabilidade civil.

not trace back to anything the physician or lab had done; both Josette and Nicolas, in fact, had contracted rubella before either the physician or the lab had even entered the picture. The real author of Nicolas' condition was, tragically but undeniably, nature. In fact, the errors of his mother's medical providers, by preventing his abortion, had (however inadvertently) saved his life. Could they possibly be penalized for this?

The final judicial act in the Perruche drama occurred in 2000, when the Court of Cassation, meeting in full plenary session, endorsed the report of Counselor Pierre Sargos and finally confirmed the defendants' civil liability to Nicolas himself for his own damages.

After the public outcry generated from this trial, in March 4th, 2002 the French Parliament passed a new legislationstating that no one is allowed to claim damages arising from the fact of being born.

In Brazil, the loss of a chance theory made its *debut* in a case tried before the State Court of *Rio Grande do Sul*, in 1990, as a result of a Myopia correction surgery that ended up causing a 2 degree hypermetropia and blurries in the operated eye[2]. The Associate Justices decided in favour of the physician, ruling that the loss of a chance theory did not apply to that particular situation.

The point of bringing up these cases is to point the relevance of the Loss of a Chance Theory in the medical responsibility field. It´s not the purpose of this brief study to discuss other areas of applicability of the theory, but only the medical implications of it, and its relations to Brazilian Law, which does not provide for any specific concept of loss of a chance.

The loss of a chance cannot be considered pain and suffering, nor actual damage. It doesn´t fit as well in the idea of profit and loss (since here it´s necessary an objective, tangible probability that the expected result would happen if not for the damage). Instead, it presents itself as an autonomous form of compensation derived from an undeniable – yet ramdomic – loss of an opportunity, where the desirable outcome cannot be guaranteed, in spite of the damage or the inaction of a third party.

In this situation, the so called chance is the possibility of a probable future benefit that integrates the faculties of action of the subject, considering a damage even when it can be difficult to estimate

2 As described in details by Sérgio Savi, in *Responsabilidade civil por perda de uma chance*, 2006, p. 45

its scope and range. In this competition of past and future factors, necessary and contingent, there is a current and certain consequence.

The idea of loss of a chance, then, rests closer to the concept of pecuniary damage than that of pain and suffering. And that leads to the question: is this theory capable of being used as a form of compensation under the current legal system in Brazil? Moreover: in a field as randomic as the medical sciences, is there space for the measurement of uncertain and unforeseeable probabilities?

2. The Brazilian Legal System regarding compensation and torts

Without a proper legal definition, one has to resort to the use of analogy to build a reasonable doctrine that can be suitable to medical cases. Regarding that, three are the main legal diplomas to take into consideration: the 2002 Civil Code, the Consumer´s Protection Act and the Medical Ethics Code.

Article 186[3] of the Brazilian Civil Code states that those who, by voluntary action or omission, negligence or recklessness, violates law and causes harm to another, albeit exclusively moral, commits an unlawful act.

Article 927[4] states that those who, by an unlawful act (articles 186 and 187), causes harm to another, is obliged to repair it.

Another important guideline comes from article 944[5], that directly determines that compensation is measured by the extent of the damage. Complementing that notion, article 951[6] states that "the provisions of arts. 948, 949 and 950 are also applicable in the case of compensation due from those who, in the exercise of their professional

3 **Art. 186.** Aquele que, por ação ou omissão voluntária, negligência ou imprudência, violar direito e causar dano a outrem, ainda que exclusivamente moral, comete ato ilícito.

4 **Art. 927.** Aquele que, por ato ilícito (arts. 186 e 187), causar dano a outrem, fica obrigado a repará-lo.

5 **Art. 944.** A indenização mede-se pela extensão do dano.

6 **Art. 951.** O disposto nos arts. 948, 949 e 950 aplica-se ainda no caso de indenização devida por aquele que, no exercício de atividade profissional, por negligência, imprudência ou imperícia, causar a morte do paciente, agravar-lhe o mal, causar-lhe lesão, ou inabilitá-lo para o trabalho.

activity, by acting with negligence, recklessness or malpractice, cause the death of the patient, aggravate his illness, cause him injury, or incapacitate him to work.

Consumer´s Defense Code, by its turn, establishes the general rule of objective liability, by ruling that the service provider answers, regardless of the existence of fault, to the repair of damages caused to consumers by defects in the provision of services, as well as by insufficient or inadequate information on their fruition and risks[7].

The fourth paragraph of the same article[8], however, expressly excludes the objective liability of health care providers when determining that their responsibility is personal, and will be assessed by verifying the presence of guilt, rejecting the concept of presumed harm.

Even the Medical Ethics Code, which in theory, should be concerned with the ethics of the medical profession, gives special attention to the damages caused to the patient, mixing ethics and civil law in a very confusing way, stating in its very first article[9] that it is forbidden to *cause damage* to the patient, by action or omission, characterized as malpractice, recklessness or negligence.

All things considered, the unavoidable conclusion is that the Brazilian legal system follows the classic model of tort and liability, focusing on the actual damage, caused by negligence, fault or an unlawful act, being far from accepting a theory in which compensation is based on the loss of a probability.

The very existence of the loss of a chance theory is based on a hypothetical uncertainty, which finds no place in a set of rules based on the compensation of actual damages, and specially in an activity as randomic as medicine.

---

7 Art. 14 – O fornecedor de serviços responde, independentemente da existência de culpa, pela reparação dos danos causados aos consumidores por defeitos relativos à prestação dos serviços, bem como por informações insuficientes ou inadequadas sobre sua fruição e riscos.

8 § 4º – A responsabilidade pessoal dos profissionais liberais será apurada mediante a verificação de culpa.

9 É vedado ao médico: Art. 1º Causar dano ao paciente, por ação ou omissão, caracterizável como imperícia, imprudência ou negligência.

3. The inadequacy of the loss of a chance theory in medical activity

Accepting the idea of compensation for medical events based on a loss of a chance means accepting the idea of a partial, semi-responsibility, where compensation can be granted considering not only the degree of uncertainty, but also the possibility that the hypothetical event would happen even without interference of the physician, rather being part of a natural development of the treatment, intervention or disease.

The single element present in this kind of relation is the damage. No direct causation can be established, nor the agent can be held responsible for an event that may or may not happen. It is, therefore, an autonomous type of compensation that cannot be considered moral damage (pain and suffering), nor an indemnity for pecuniary damages.

The lost chance can be divided in two types in here: the loss of future opportunities, and a future loss of opportunities. The first one is a present treat. The second, an exercise of futurology. And here is the deadlock: if the damage is present, real, and measurable, there is no need for a compensation for a lost chance. Compensation can be calculated and determined by the real extent of the damage caused.

We are not advocating for the extinction of the loss of a chance theory. It is a valid form of conflict resolution, and even a necessary one for several situations outside the medical field. But again, one cannot deny that this is not an appropriate answer to dilemas that arise from a medical situation, naturally and intrinsecally filled with uncertainty and without any guarantee of results, no matter how soon the illness was discovered, how state-of-the art were the hospital facilities, how adequate was the proposed treatment according to medical litterature, or how skilled the physician was.

Some might say that a loss of a chance can be measured in cases where a wrong diagnosis causes damages to a patient, making it impossible to treat a disease that has reached a point of no return, or even causing the patient´s death. Again, what needs to be considered here is the fact that a misdiagnosis can be divided in those evident and those hard to assess.

But even when the diagnosis is "easy" and evident, it is virtually impossible to predict or determine how it influenced in the outcome of the situation. Medicine is not an exact science, and even if the some damage can be measured from the misdiagnosis, it is the case to compensate for an actual damage, or pecuniary damage. If the damage is hypothetical (a chance "lost"), and there is no way to establish the nexus of causality between the physician´s fault and how the situation developed, there are no legal grounds (again, in Brazilian Law) for conviction and compensation based on the loss of a chance.

The same goes for those hypothesis where exams are delayed, or interventions postponed. If from this inaction results an actual damage, it must be compensated properly, and the legal system already has rules for it. If the damage is not measurable, or worse, there is just the possibility of a future damage, it cannot be guaranteed – given the uncertainty of the medical activity, that it will occur, and that it wouldn´t occur just the same, regardless of the physician´s inertia. Therefore, in a system that requires damage to establish compensations, there is no place for indemnizatons based on the loss of a chance theory.

Another situation is when the lack of information contributes to a bad outcome. The patient is convinced that there is no alternate possibility and agrees to undergo a certain treatment suggested by the doctor, and loses the opportunity of trying something less invasive (although more expensive) or maybe an experimental treatment that has been showing optmistic results in other patients (although inconclusive regarding the percentage of success that could be expected).

Again, this is not the case for a conviction for loss of a chance. It´s rather a case of informational negligence, and can be examined properly under a lawsuit based on lack of (or inappropriate) information.

The Brazilian Consumer´s Defense Code states, in its article 6,[10] that one of the basic consumer rights are: III – adequate and clear information on the different products and services, with a correct specification of quantity, characteristics, composition, quality, incidental taxes and price, as well as the risks they present.

The information, to be "appropriate", does NOT need to meet the doctor´s assessment of the situation, but the patient´s. All relevant data, alternatives (even those the physician thinks are not recommended to the case, based on its experience) and risks must be

10 Art. 6º São direitos básicos do consumidor:
III – a informação adequada e clara sobre os diferentes produtos e serviços, com especificação correta de quantidade, características, composição, qualidade, tributos incidentes e preço, bem como sobre os riscos que apresentem;

disclosed to the patient, in an understandable way, in order to provide sufficient elements for a decision – a choice – to be made.

A treatment or procedure can be considered successful from a clinical point of view, but later seen as inappropriate when confronted with other possible outcomes that could be expected if a different therapeutic method had been informed to – and chosen by – the patient.

This lack of information doesn´t necessarily means negligence. It may represent the expression of the physicians beliefs, based in his own experience or in the medical literature, that the proposed solution was the most adequate to the situation faced at a given moment.

The problem is that this behavior goes against ethical principles and legal commands that consider mandatory the disclosure of all information available. Withholding information about alternatives may be considered – in a lawsuit or in a disciplinary investigation – an undue interference in treatment, thus breaching confidence and contrary to the principles of good-faith and autonomy.

In Brazil, the Superior Court of Justice (STJ) also decided in favor of the plaintiff, helding a blood bank liable for lack of proper communication of test results (REsp nº 1.071.969/PE).

In 2007, another case, involving plastic surgery (AgRg in Ag 818.144/SP) had a similar result, with the court ruling that "the physician who do not inform his patient about the risks of surgery is negligent, being liable for all damages resulting from the intervention".

In the opposite direction, a case judged in 2009 (REsp 1.051.674/RS) exempted the doctor from being considered responsible for an unexpected result, because he proved the fulfillment of the duty to inform.

Another recent case, originated from the Justice Court of the State of Minas Gerais (Civil Appeal n. 1.0223.08.246703-4/001), and ruled in 2013, help in the task of defining the consequences of informational negligence. It refers to a litigation between a patient and his dentist. The dentist was forced to pay the patient a compensation for moral damages, due to a fracture caused in the patient´s jaw, during a tooth extraction procedure. Compensation was not granted as a direct result of the fracture, which was proved to be a potential risk of that particular treatment, but because the dentist failed to fulfill his duty to inform the patient about the risks inherent to that kind of procedure.

And why is this so intrinsecally different? Regarding medical responsibility, one cannot compensate for a partial damage. It´s about another kind of damage: a lost chance. An *opportunity* that was lost, and *not* the expected benefit in itself.

Imagine, once again, the situation where a surgical procedure was delayed, an exam was not ordered, or proper information was not given at the correct time. All these can generate actual and present damages, fully capable of being compensated in court. But based on a different ground, not on the lost opportunity, simply because there is no safe way to guarantee, or even to establish that, if the surgical procedure had taken place, the exam performed, or information delivered in a timely manner, they would be responsible for an eventual success of the treatment, given a plethora of casual and unpredictable circumstances, so vivid and omnipresent in the medical practice.

In other words, no level of liability can arise from such hypothetical uncertainty. A court is not prepared to determine whether a bad outcome ocurred because of a lost opportunity or as a natural result of the illness or pathology. There are too many variables – some of them unknown to the doctor or to the patient – to place such responsibility over the healthcare provider´s shoulder.

Medical responsibility requires the existence of an unlawful act, negligence, recklessness, malpractice. And these are measurable (and punishable) by other forms of compensation in tort law. A random circumstance, the loss of a possibility of cure or chance of treatment that cannot be controlled by the physician does not constitute civil liability. A basic requirement for liability in the medical field is fault. Uncertainty and hipothetical scenarios are not enough to replace it.

Of course, not all cases can be excluded from the analysis under the loss of a chance theory, but they are related to the medical *activity*, not the medical *practice*.

Let´s take, for instance, the hipothesis of a stem cells bank, responsible for the storage of umbilical cords. For any given reason, these umbilical cords disappear, get misplaced, or useless for its purposes due to bad storage conditions.

In this case, it would be possible to establish the extent of pecuniary damages, to calculate an adittional compensation for pain and suffering, and also determine an autonomous compensation for the loss of a chance of using the stem cells for treatment in the future, considering there is a measurable, direct causation between the opportunity lost and the negligence of the stem cells bank.

This example illustrates perfectly the point we are advocating, against the possibility of compensating chance. From the scientific point of view, the full range of stem cells use and efficacy is still unknown. And yet, an indemnization based on the chance lost will be covering something not just hypothetical, but maybe (another uncertainty here) non-existant.

Civil liability already deals with the problem, considering it a breach of contract, which has an entirely different approach, promoting damage compensation in a much more efficient way, with much clearer borders.

Another possibility takes place when medical reports or medical exams from one patient are misplaced with those from a third part, thus preventing this person from competing in a tournament, or being accepted in a job selection process, or even from starting a treatment, based on someone else´s medical history.

However, these are borderline cases. And there is no direct medical intervention in the examples above, but only poor planning and bad administrative execution, resulting in a faulty service. The fact that these situations can occur in a healthcare related environment is merely incidental, and does not invalidate the previous statements. The best efforts, expertise and due diligence of the healthcare professional will always find a natural nemesis in the limitations of science, and the unpredictability of the human body.

4. An analysis on recent jurisprudential developments

Some examples of what can happen when legal concepts are not properly employed in lawsuits are not hard to find. The following narrative will concentrate on how dangerous it is when judicial decisivos produce a lack of stability.

In 2003, the State Court of Rio de Janeiro[11] decided a case where the plaintiffs sued a maternitiy hospital claiming that negligence was

11 TJRJ Embargos Infringentes n. 00446/2002 Embargantes: Valter Franco Braga e Dulce Rodrigues Ribas. Embargada: Casa de Saúde e Maternidade São José Ltda. Rio de Janeiro, 03.06.2003. Available at www.tjrj.jus.br

responsible for the death of their newborn child. The boy, while still in nursery and only after 18 hours after birth, presented apnea and cardiorespiratory arrest, and was left unattended for nearly two hours before being taken to a neonatal ICU, compromising thus his chances of survival.

The court recognized that the hospital failed to deliver proper medical care, and that the baby lost his best chances of survival, and that his death could have been avoided were the medical staff more efficient and less negligent with the first response. After the loss of a chance was established, the court ruled in favour of the plaintiffs, granting an indemnization for both parents, on the grounds of moral damages and pain and suffering.

The lack of technique is evident, since loss of a chance and moral damages represent two different kinds of compensation, and one cannot be granted under the recognition of the other. That denotes a misunderstanding of the grounds for tort law.

A second case was tried at the same State Court in Rio de Janeiro[12] in 2007. After perceiving an abnormality in his right eye, a patient sought hospital care, and retinal displacement was diagnosed, requiring urgent intervention.

The public hospital did not have the necessary resources, and a consultation was scheduled for two days later at another hospital. Because no doctor was available there, the appointment was scheduled again for five days later. A treatment was started, and the need for surgical intervention was recognized, but authorization for the procedure came only four months later when the patient had already lost sight of his right eye.

The court acknowledged that the delay in carrying out the procedure was responsible for rendering it ineffective, without the least possibility of success, applying, therefore, the theory of loss of a chance of cure, condemning the hospital to the payment of moral damages, but only partially, because, the court ruled, it was impossible to be certain of the success of the surgical intervention, were it performed at the appropriate time.

12 TJRJ Apelação Cível n. 2006.001.08137. Apelantes: Guaraciaba Barbosa e Hospital do Olho. Apelados: os mesmos. Rio de Janeiro, 2007. Available at www.tjrj.jus.br

Again, the two institutes of civil liability were mistakenly confused, creating an indemnity based on different grounds from those demanded in the lawsuit.

In 2009, the Superior Court of Justice,[13] reexamining a case from the State Court of Rio Grande do Sul, in which a patient died due to surgical complications, ruled in favour of the defendant recognizing in its decision that the loss of a chance theory applies only to cases in which the damage is real, actual and certain, within a probability analysis, and not just a mere possibility, since the potential or uncertain damage, under tort law, is not compensable.[14]

Another case ruled in 2013, by the State Court of Rio Grande do Sul[15], analyzed the situation of a seven-year-old child who suffered a head injury after falling from a five meters height and was medicated without a proper craniectomy to determine the extent of the injury. Even though the child remained under medical observation for 17 hours, the lack of adequate treatment left the child with permanent lesions.

The court recognized the possibility of applying the theory of loss of chance, and condemned the doctors and the hospital to the payment of compensation for moral damages, in addition to treatment expenses.

One last case worth bringing up is also from 2013,[16] in which the same Superior Court of Justice, paradoxically, decided to reexamine a

13 STJ – REsp 1104665 RS 2008/0251457-1, Brasília, judged in 09.06.2009, by the Third Chamber, and published in DJe 04.08.2009. Available at www.stj.jus.br

14 Extracted from the original ruling: "...III – A chamada "teoria da perda da chance", de inspiração francesa e citada em matéria de responsabilidade civil, aplica-se aos casos em que o dano seja real, atual e certo, dentro de um juízo de probabilidade, e não de mera possibilidade, porquanto o dano potencial ou incerto, no âmbito da responsabilidade civil, em regra, não é indenizável; IV – In casu, o v. acórdão recorrido concluiu haver mera possibilidade de o resultado morte ter sido evitado caso a paciente tivesse acompanhamento prévio e contínuo do médico no período pós-operatório, sendo inadmissível, pois, a responsabilização do médico com base na aplicação da ´teoria da perda da chance´."

15 TJRS Apelação Cível n. 70052376779, 9th Civil Chamber, ruled in 27.02.2013. Available at www.tjrs.jus.br

16 STJ REsp 1254.14 – PR, ruled in 04.12.2012 and published in 20.02.2013. Available at www.stj.jus.br

case originating from the State Court of Paraná, and ruled that it was valid to apply the loss of a chance theory.

The case was about an inadequate oncological treatment, that reduced the possibilities of cure for the patient, and that this loss of chance constituted an autonomous damage. In spite of these conclusions, the Court acknowledged that there was uncertainty in the doctor's participation in the outcome, and that the damage might have been caused by the disease, and not by the inadequate treatment itself.

These mixed signs, and contradictory rulings do not contribute to the development of a theory adapted to the national legal framework regarding civil liability. On the contrary, they increase uncertainty by allowing each of the different state courts to develop a particular understanding, and equally dissociated from good legal technique.

5. Conclusions

The conceptual idea of civil liability does not communicate with that one expressed in the theory of the loss of a chance.

In medical practice, the occurrence of an injury, a damage, and fault for malpractice, are already punishable by the existing legal framework, which are the pillars of civil liability established in federal legislation.

For all the above arguments, it is clear that the loss of a chance theory does not find shelter in this legal framework, which already has adequate forms of establishing compensation mechanisms for damages originated from the medical practice.

The courts have adopted the conceptual idea of this theory, using it in a wrong way, recognizing its existence and validity, therefore embracing it, but using it to justify condemnation in other types of indemnization, for pain and suffering, moral damages or actual damages.

Civil liability and *loss of a chance* are, therefore, contradictory elements. The first one deals with real damages, while the latter faces a greyish zone due to the uncertainty of the medical sciences, the unique characteristics of each disease, and the idiosyncrasy of each patient, which precludes the possibility of establishing any reasonable doubt, sufficiently palpable to determine whether there was competition from the medical act for the occurrence of the bad outcome or if this was only the result of mere iatrogeny.

If the Brazilian courts wish to treat Loss of a Chance as an autonomous kind of damage in the healthcare field, they must be prepared to develop sufficient, convincing arguments to recognize the existence of an autonomous condemnation, separate from moral damages, and with its own means of calculating, not a partial compensation, but the exact measure of the opportunity (the chance) that was lost.

Without these safeguards, an awkard situation will occur; one in which a foreign legal theory was adopted, but remained orphaned.

6. References

ALCOZ, Luis Medina. *Hacia una nueva teoría general de la causalidad en la responsabilidad civil contractual (y extracontractual): La doctrina de la pérdida de oportunidades. In*, Revista de Responsabilidad Civil y Seguro, n. 30, Madrid, 2009, pp. 31-74.

BÉNÉJAT, Murielle. *L´autonomie de la responsabilité médicale pour défaut d´information (À propos de quelques arrêts rendus em 2010)*, *in* Revue Générale de Droit Médical, 38, Les Études Hopitaliéres, Bordeaux, 2011.

BIONDI, Eduardo Abreu. Teoria da perda de uma chance na responsabilidade civil. 24.06.2008. Availableat http:direitonet.com.br/ artigos/ exibir/3988/teoria-da-perda-de-uma-chance-na-responsabilidade-civil

BRAZIL, Lei 8.078/90. Código de Defesa do Consumidor. Diário Oficial da União, 12.09.1990.

BRAZIL, Lei 10.406/02. Código Civil Brasileiro. Diário Oficial da União, 11.01.2002.

BRAZIL, STJ – REsp 1104665 RS 2008/0251457-1, Brasília, judged in 09.06.2009, by the Third Chamber, and published in DJe 04.08.2009. Available at www.stj.jus.br

BRAZIL, STJ REsp 1254.14 – PR, Brasília, ruled in 04.12.2012 and published in 20.02.2013. Available at www.stj.jus.br

BRAZIL, TJRJ Apelação Cível n. 2006.001.08137. Apelantes: Guaraciaba Barbosa e Hospital do Olho. Apelados: os mesmos. Rio de Janeiro, 2007. Available at www.tjrj.jus.br

BRAZIL, TJRJ Embargos Infringentes n. 00446/2002 Embargantes: Valter Franco Braga e Dulce Rodrigues Ribas. Embargada: Casa de Saúde e Maternidade São José Ltda. Rio de Janeiro, 03.06.2003. Available at www.tjrj.jus.br

BRAZIL, TJRS Apelação Cível n. 70052376779, 9th Civil Chamber, ruled in 27.02.2013. Available at www.tjrs.jus.br

CARNAÚBA, Daniel Amaral. Responsabilidade civil pela perda de uma chance – A álea e a técnica. Método, São Paulo, 2013.

CONSELHO FEDERAL DE MEDICINA, Resolução CFM nº 1931/2009. Código de Ética Médica. Diário Oficial da União, 17.09.2009.

DANTAS, Eduardo. Les différences entre le consentement informé et le choix éclairé comme causes d´exclusion de responsabilité civile dans la relation médecin-patient. L´autonomie du patient face au droit brésilien, in Revue générale de droit medical, n. 29, Les Études Hospitalières, Bordeaux, pp. 125-147, 2008.

FRANCE. *L´Affair Perruche*. Cour de Cassation, Assemblée plénière, du 17 novembre 2000, 99-13.701, available at

https://www.legifrance.gouv.fr/affichJuriJudi.do?idTexte=JURITEXT000007041543&dateTexte=

PALLARÉS, Eduardo Asensi; CLARES, Iñigo Cid-Luna. *La evolución de la doctrina de la pérdida de oportunidade em responsabilidade médica, in* Revista CESCO de Derecho de Consumo, n. 8/2013, pp. 228-239, viewed at https://www.revista.uclm.es/index.php/cesco/article/viewFile/416/358.

RAPOSO, Vera Lúcia. Do ato médico ao problema jurídico. Almedina, Coimbra, 2013.

________. *Em busca da chance perdida. O dano da perda de chance, em especial na responsabilidade médica. In,* Revista do Ministério Público, 138: Abril: Junho 2014 (pp. 09-61). Portugal.

ROCHA, Nuno Santos. A perda da chance como uma nova espécie de dano. Almedina, Coimbra, 2015.

ROSÁRIO, Grácia Cristina Moreira do. A perda da chance de cura na responsabilidade civil médica. Lúmen Juris, Rio de Janeiro, 2009.

SAVI, Sérgio. Responsabilidade civil por perda de uma chance. Atlas, São Paulo, 2006.

SILVA, Rafael Peteffi da. Responsabilidade civil pela perda de uma chance. Atlas, São Paulo, 2007.

YONG, Samuel; YONG, Camilo A. Rodríguez. *Perdida de Oportunidad*, *in* Revista Virtual Via Inveniendi Et Iudicandi. Edición 12, Vol. 6, n. 2, julio – diciembre, 2011

III

LEGAL ASPECTS OF *POST-MORTEM* REPRODUCTION. A COMPARATIVE PERSPECTIVE OF FRENCH, BRAZILIAN AND PORTUGUESE LEGAL SYSTEMS

Eduardo Dantas

Abstract: Death arrives always too soon, and most often unexpectedly, destroying our plans and the plans of the ones who love us. Medically assisted reproduction offers nowadays a technique that makes possible to have children from someone that recently passed away. Post mortem reproduction is not the satisfaction of a mere whim, but the continuity of strong love affections, and frequently provides some kind of fulfillment to the common aspiration of the couple in constituting a family. All around the world courts and law makers are profoundly divided in the legitimacy of this practice. The well being of the child to be and the respect for the dead person seem to be the strongest arguments against. But, as this study will show, none of them resist to a more careful scrutiny. Therefore, not only post mortem embryo transfer should be allowed, but post mortem insemination and fertilization should also be permitted.

Keywords: Medically assisted reproduction; post-mortem reproduction; consent; right to constitute a family.

1. INTRODUCTION

The last five decades have witnessed an extremely fast development in the field of medical sciences, with effects that have not yet been properly measured. The scientists´ achievements, undoubtedly prove to be important for the development of society, generating behavioral changes in the social fabric, and in society as a whole.

These changes, of course, demand for adjustments in the legal system, and the law is necessarily slower on its way to provide solutions, or even regulate certain acts and procedures, thus causing conflicts and doubts arising from the evolution of the way we face the world.

The lack of adequate legal means to respond to these emerging conflicts leaves to bioethics, and to the systemic interpretation of the sources of law, the task of pointing out the new paths to be followed, strengthening the communication of such different sciences, and yet so interrelated as law and medicine.

One of the situations that well illustrates the difficulty in finding the correct path between the alternatives is well defined by the ethical-legal conflicts arising from the possibility of post-mortem assisted reproduction.

Recently, two cases caught the attention of the Brazilian press, involving post-mortem reproduction. The first case[1] reported a judicial pilgrimage of a woman – Nara Azzolini – who lost her fiance – Bruno Leite – because of an aneurysm that killed him within a few hours. On receiving the news of impending death, Nara and Bruno's parents decided in mutual agreement, to seek for the services of a fertility center to harvest sperm from Bruno, in order to follow up the future marrying couple´s plans to generate children from their union.

Guided by the clinic´s staff, they sought – and obtained – a court order (in less than 12 hours) to perform surgical procedure that removed tissue from Bruno´s testicles, which was then frozen, a technique that can make them viable for about 20 years, according to scientific estimates.

The next step, described the newspaper the report, would be to get permission to conceive a child through *in vitro* fertilization with the use of the dead groom´s genetic material. This situation, in addition to bioethical dilemmas, raised other legal issues because of the absence of an specific legislation on the subject, raising further doubts about which way to go because of the consequences of inheritance, equity, and psychological matters.

We must take into consideration the fact there is no living will or any kind of anticipated declaration of intent or similar document, recording in writing the desire of the late groom to see a child conceived after his death.

---

1 Avaiable at Portal G1 (www.g1.com.br) and reproduced on the website Espaço Vital (www.espacovital.com.br) on April 26, 2010.

A few days later, the newspaper *Folha de São Paulo*[2] reported the injunction granted by the 13th Civil Court of Curitiba / PR – Case No. 0027862-73.2010.8.16.0001 – authorizing the school teacher Katia Lenemeier to go to a fertilization procedure, trying to get pregnant with the frozen sperm of her late husband, who died three months before, due to melanoma. Having been surprised by the appearance and fast development of the disease, the couple – married for five years – decided to seek expert medical help to freeze the semen of the husband before the start of chemotherapy, which could lead him to infertility as a side-effect.

Seeking to continue the project that they shared, Mrs. Lenemeier sought the laboratory where the harvesting and storage had been carried out for insemination procedures to begin, occasion when she was informed by that institution that she could not use it, since there was no prior consent of the deceased husband, releasing the use after his death.

Because of the refusal, she filed a lawsuit, obtaining a court order that authorized the use of the frozen material, filling a legal void.

These and other cases, until a few years ago, would be considered science fiction, but they are becoming ordinary, requiring a clear legislative position in order to dispel doubts and normalize the situation, establishing what legal parameters and ethical limits should be followed in similar situations.

The purpose of this brief study is therefore to determine the legal aspects surrounding the concepts of *in vitro* fertilization *post-mortem*, placing them in historical perspective, and analyzing them under French, Brazilian and Portuguese laws, seeking to identify solutions and proposals of path to be followed.

For that to be achieved, it is necessary to clarify some technical aspects.

2. *Post-mortem* Reproduction

Reproduction *post-mortem* may take the form of insemination, fertilization or embryo transfer.

2 Edition of May 25, 2010.

The first and second hypotheses are particularly controversial, especially when there is no authorization of the male element for his sperm to be used for reproductive purposes.

In the third case there was necessarily a consent of the male element, which first allowed the use of his sperm for fertilization of oocytes from the wife or partner. However, this consent was given, as a rule, so that the process was conducted while he was alive, so the question is whether it would remain valid if the man knew he would die soon, and his child were to be born after that time.

In fact, all cases that come before us relate to the death of the male partner, and the female´s subsequent desire to use his sperm or embryos created from it. But theoretically, it can also arise in the opposite situation, and be the man who wants to use the oocytes of the deceased, or embryos generated with her oocytes, using a surrogate mother's womb or even his new companion´s womb. But here, we will not look into this situation of *post-mortem* reproduction.

Not only because the complications relating to this hypothesis are much more intricate (remember, first, that it will always be the need for a surrogate mother, at least, to transfer the embryos into the uterus of the new partner of the surviving male, which will always hurt some sensibilities), but also because the statutory regimes which allow, to some extent, *post-mortem* reproduction appear to have only envisaged the death of the male.

There is no social consensus, nor religious, nor legally, on this practice, because there are laws that allow on certain conditions (Netherlands, Greece, United Kingdom or Belgium), others that strictly prohibit it (Italy, France), and many others saying nothing in this respect (Brazil).

In addition to the many ethical problems that arise, and that will be addressed here, two more practical issues arise right before our eyes: in one hand, the establishment of parentage, on the other, the issues of hereditary succession.

With regard to the hereditary issue[3], especially in Portugal, the problem arises because the related laws were written assuming that the successors were alive, or about to be born by the time of death of the deceased, and could be identifiable at that moment, especially

3 ZANELATTO, Marco Antonio, "Fertilização Artificial...", pp. 53-59.

by medicine, with the time of uterine implantation, not fertilization. The admittance of inheritance rights of these newly created (and unexpected) would-be-heirs could introduce here a breach for legal uncertainty, which would be extremely dangerous. But on the other hand, denying them succession rights would imply discrimination against children based on the conditions of birth, which is legally forbidden in Portugal and Brazil.

Regarding the issue of paternity, with a prior consent of the father – and that serves as recognition of paternity – the child would be considered, for all legal purposes, as his son or daughter. And it seems that even without such consent the solution might not be different (at least considering Portuguese laws), lest the child be deprived of legal father.

2.1. *Insemination / fertilization* post-mortem

Let's talk first of the situations in which the woman is inseminated or fertilized with semen from a man already dead, as a rule, her husband.

This practice is usually banned in legal systems because it is considered interference in the dignity of the deceased,[4] by tampering with his genetic material without a living will that could serve as a support. Cumulatively, the "greed factor" of the widow should be taken into account. The possibility of trying to generate an additional source of livelihood derived from the assets of the deceased spouse by giving birth to a son as an ultimate source of income, given the central role it can play in terms of distribution of assets and goods.[5]

However, we believe that – in the overwhelming majority of cases – what drives these women is a sense totally opposed to this: its the love for the deceased, who hoped to share his life. What remains is the possibility to try to overcome his absence with the birth of a much-desired son.

Admitting the *post-mortem* insemination – and it seems that this is a good solution – it will need, however, to meet certain requirements,

4 FERRAZ, Sérgio. "Manipulações biológicas...", p. 29.

5 CARCABA FERNÁNDEZ, Maria. "Problemas jurídicos planteados...", p. 82.

parallel to the taxes for the living will:[6] i) based upon the wishes of the deceased, which should be expressed in writing; ii) to perform within a specified period after the death of a spouse or partner.

The trend of national laws and international diplomas is to prohibit this practice[7]. However, the fundamental right to a family will always be invoked in order to allow it, because, somehow, it is the woman's desire to extend the family lost with the death of her husband (although not all authors accept the argument in these terms).[8]

As in many other medical issues of law, it is whether we should stick to the strict rule of consent, seeking for a greater security, or, rather, it is preferable to choose the solution that best meets the supposed interest of the one that is unable to consent, despite all the risks that this implies. Does the marriage contract implies a concomitant commitment to breed, whatever the future circumstances, even if they involve the disappearance of the alleged father?

2.1.1. The leading cases

It is in France that we find most of the judicial rulings on this issue, and these rulings have defined the European trends in this field.

In the 80's, the famous Parpalaix Case,[9] the High Court of Créteil was called upon to decide the claim of a widow who, coupled with her in-laws, demanded the sperm bank where her late husband had previously stored his semen, in order to be inseminated. Since her husband had taken this decision after being informed that he suffered a testicular cancer, the court found that such behavior could be taken as tacit consent to its use *post-mortem*, this presumption supported by

---

6 About living wills, see Roberto ANDORNO, Nikola BILLER-ANDORNO, Susanne BRAUER, "Advance Health Care Directives…", p. 207/227; André PEREIRA, *O Consentimento Informado…*, p. 240 ss.; André PEREIRA, "Advance Directives…", p. 165/171.

7 However, article 9/2 of the Spanish Law (Law 14/2006, May 26) admits *post mortem* insemination, if preceded by the husband´s written consent.

8 Rejecting it, for inadequacy, Cristina CAMPIGLIO, "*Procreazione Assistita e Famiglia...*", p. 149.

9 Court ruling from August 1st, 1984, High Court of Creteil. Cfr. Nathalie MASSAGER, *Les Droits de l'Enfant à Naitre*, p. 433 ss.

the fact that the bank sperm never have informed that their practice was to not return the genetic material after the death of the depositor.

Another interesting issue discussed here relates to the legal status of the contract in question. The Court held that it was not a deposit contract (because the sperm was not a response that could be the subject of such agreement), nor with the contract of organ donation, but a *sui generis* contract, for therapeutic purposes.

Some years later the High Court of Toulouse[10] – ruling over a decision on the appeal of a woman at the center where the deceased husband's sperm was deposited to be returned to him – concentrated on the contract classification that had been proposed by the Court of Creteil. The difference, compared to the previous case here, is the fact that the man had signed a document which expressly stipulated that the sperm could only be used in his presence and with his consent, and therefore the court of Toulouse disregarded the request of the applicant and ordered the destruction of the sperm, considered "une sécrétion contenant le germe de la vie et destinée à la procréation d'un être humain".

Note that the court's decision was not based on the general condemnation of this practice (although it revealed concerns about the paternity of children born that way), but the existence of that clause, which could even have been revoked by the implied will of the deceased, to the extent that the content of contracts can not be unilaterally amended or repealed, based on the principles of contract law. Still, the question remains whether one could not apply the rules of inheritance and consider the widow the heir of the deceased husband's sperm, as some years later a U.S. court in California came to understand in the case *Hecht v. Superior Court.*[11]

Still in France, the same court of Creteil ruled again on a *post-mortem* insemination case.[12] This time, although it has classified the contract as a deposit (concurrently, the sperm was legally qualified as a "thing"), the court paradoxically refused to surrender it to the wife, as would happen if it were a genuine contract of deposit. We assume

10 Court ruling from March 26, 1991, High Court of Toulouse.

11 Case *Hecht v. Superior Court* 20 Cal. Rptr. 2d 275 (Ct. App. 1993).

12 Court ruling from April 4, 1995, High Court of Creteil.

that the reason is that, to date, have effect in art. 152.-L 2 of the *Code de la Santé Publique*, in the formulation given by Law 94-654, which stipulates, among the requirements for those who want to be beneficiaries of assisted reproductive techniques, that both parents are alive at the time of the procedure.

But *Blood*[13] is the case that serves as one of the leading cases in this regard so far. The story is summarized as follows: Mr. Blood had initiated a reproductive treatment with his wife when he suddenly fell into a coma before he could even leave some written document. Never came out of it, but before he died his wife gave orders for his semen to be extracted for insemination, already anticipating the dream of having children that they shared in common. The process was carried out, but with the opposition of the Human Fertilization Embryology Authority, the entity responsible for overseeing the British reproductive procedures ethically complex. Because this collection of sperm did not meet the legal requirements, in particular, lacked the prior consent of Mr. Blood. Therefore, not only the realization of *post-mortem* insemination at an English clinic was denied, but it was also refused to allow the sperm to be taken to another country where the procedure was permitted.

The query appeared before the English High Court, where Mrs. Blood invoked the Communitarian regime for the freedom to provide services (Articles 49 et seq. of the Treaty of Rome) to justify the application of this reproductive treatment in another country which authorized it. Their reasoning was based on the jurisprudence of the Court of Justice according to which the freedom to provide services not only takes advantage of those providing them, but also those who want to receive, guidance also applies to medical services (*Luisi and*

---

13 Case *Regina v. Human Fertilisation and Embriology Authority, ex parte Blood* [1997] 2 AII ER 687, *Court of Appeal,* commented by Jean-Sylvestre BERGÉ, "Tourisme Procréatif et Droit Communautaire… , p. 599 ss.; Ruth DEECH, "Losing Control…", p. 582 ss; John HARRIS, "Rights and Reproductive Choice", p. 16 ss; Brigitta LURGER, "Fortpflanzugsmedizin und Abstammungsrecht", p. 113, 114; J. K. MASON, R.A. SMITH, G. T. LAURIE, *Law and Medical Ethics*, p. 72/74; Tony McGLEENAN, "Reproductive Technology…" , p. 277/280; Françoise SHENFIELD, "Panorama de la Reproducción...", p. 281/283.

Carbone Case).[14] Although it could always be argued based on the free movement of goods (Article 28 et seq. of the Treaty of Rome), as the animal semen had been considered for the purposes of Communitarian law, as a commodity[15], although it is arguable that human semen can meet the Community definition of "biens appréiables en argent et susceptibles comme tels d'être l'object de transactions commerciales" (Case *Community v. Italie*).[16] But the issue was not even raised since the thesis of freedom to provide services prevailed.

It is true that the High Court expressed some misgivings over the possibility of the Community legal system thereby allow the violation of a prohibition in English law. In contrast, the Court of Appeal had no such qualms, giving primacy to Community freedoms and therefore the claim of Mrs. Blood, who was so authorized to carry the husband's sperm to Belgium, where she was successfully inseminated. She has now two children resulting from this process.

2.1.2. Issues relating to consent

Several questions are raised concerning the consent left by the deceased for the use of his sperm:

> i) To what extent is that the death should prevent the reproduction process to a greater extent than when it occurs within a sexual reproduction? If in the latter the "disappearance" of the father after fertilization becomes irrelevant, it is appropriate that their presence is seen as decisive in assisted reproduction?
> ii) There shall be implied consent to admit here, for example, in the form of prior treatment *in vitro* fertilization, or "deposit" in a sperm bank under the same conditions, although in either case the patient had been previously

---

14 Case *Luisi and Carbone,* decisions 286/82 and 26/83, from January 31, 1984, Communitarian Court of Justice.

15 About sperm importation/exportation, Ruth DEECH, "Losing Control...", p. 588 ss.

16 Case *Community. v. Italie*, decision 7/68, from December 10, 1968, Communitarian Court of Justice.

informed of his lethal disease? Could be used here the same criterion of presumed consent as it is in criminal law[17]?
iii) And what if it is the case of heterologous reproduction? Must it still be prevented if the sperm donation had previously been agreed by the couple?
iv) In the case of consent, what are their requirements of validity? Particular formalities are required for public recognition?
v) Is the consent subjected to the same specified period of validity as a living will? May this period be extended by the consent form?
vi) Existing expiry date, this means that if fertilization is performed after that date, paternity can not be declared, leaving the child without a father?

2.2. Transfer *post-mortem*

This hypothesis[18] is less controversial, because in this case the embryos are already fertilized, being transferred to the mother´s womb after the physical disappearance of the father.

Still, it is not free from controversy. In a case that became known as the case of the "widow of Toulouse," a woman whose husband had died claimed the hospital where they had both agreed to cryopreserve their embryos to deliver them for subsequent embryo transfer. Through two controversial decisions[19] the French judicial authorities decided that the embryos should be destroyed, arguing that after the death of her

17 Article 39/2, of the Portuguese Criminal Code: "Há consentimento presumido quando a situação em que o agente actua permitir razoavelmente supor que o titular do interesse juridicamente protegido teria eficazmente consentido no facto, se conhecesse as circunstâncias em que este é praticado."

18 Judit SÁNDOR ("Reproduction and Genetics…p. 117) refers to this possibility as the "right to a continuation of a reproductive treatment". Yet about this issue, it is recommended reading, Judit SÁNDOR, "Reproductive Rights in the Hungarian Law…", p. 196 ss.

19 Ruling from May 11, 1993, High Court of Toulouse, first chamber; Ruling from April 18, 1994, Appelation Court of Toulouse, commented in Nathalie MASSAGER, *Les Droits de l'Enfant à Naitre*, p. 702 ss.

husband the woman failed to meet the requirements stipulated by the French legal system to authorize access to reproductive technologies, in particular, the presence of a father. This is because, according to the French regime regarding assisted reproductive techniques, these can not be used to overcome reproductive obstacles resulting from family backgrounds that do not correspond to the traditional model consisting of a father and a mother, but, rather, its use is admissible only to deal with problems of infertility or risk of disease transmission hereditarily transmitted. This means that the base will always be a therapeutic purpose, which seemed nonexistent here (although it is certain that at the time the couple had decided to use these techniques, such requirement was actually present).

To enhance this decision was the agreement between the couple and the hospital, which included a clause stipulating that embryos could be transferred only with the consent and presence of both members of the couple. Finally, it was invoked the emotional fragility that the widow was under, due to her husband's death, which could make her less able to raise and educate a child.

Again in France, but this time by decision of the *Tribunal de Grande Instance* of Rennes,[20] the *post-mortem* embryo transfer was rejected one more time due to the absence of consent of the deceased father.

To demonstrate that there is no sufficient consensus regarding this matter, there´s a decision ruled by the Court of Angers,[21] authorizing the transfer of embryos in a similar situation, and also allowing the child to be legally recognized as the child of the deceased and allowing him to adopt the family surname.

However, a couple of years later this practice was considered unacceptable again, this time by a higher court, the *Cour de Cassation.*[22] Between this decision and those others mentioned above was issued an opinion from the French National Ethics Council[23] in order to

20 Ruling from June 30, 1993.

21 Ruling from November 10, 1992, Tribunal de Grande Instance d'Angers, First Chamber.

22 Ruling from January 9, 1996, Cour de Cassation.

23 Opinion dated December 17, 1993, issued by the French National Ethics Council.

allow the transfer *post-mortem*, but in the meantime came the above-mentioned Law 94-654,[24] which expressly forbade it, so and instead of the earlier trials, based on a mere judicial review, here the Court of Cassation was already subjected to a legal prohibition.[25]

The legal admissibility of *post-mortem* transfer of embryos is to be based essentially on two reasons. First, because otherwise the solution will lead to the destruction of embryos (unless the donation / adoption of embryos enters the scene), so enabling its transfer is the solution that allows birth and thus most respects life.[26] Incidentally, a similar argument was invoked by the applicant in presenting the case before the *Cour de Cassation,* mentioning the provisions contained in the law of January 17, 1975, which regulates the status of pregnancy termination in French law, establishing the assumptions on what is and what is not legitimate.

In this case, it was alleged that the refusal to transfer the embryos would constitute an unlawful termination of pregnancy. But it lacks grounding to this argument because, strictly speaking, the opposition to embryo transfer did not prevent the continuation of a pregnancy, but its beginning. Even the argument of "*infant conceptus*", close to this and also called into question by the applicant, could bring some benefit, because it only aims at the protection of human heritage that actually comes to birth, allowing it to benefit from effects property previously set, giving retroactive effect to the birth,

But besides those, there are other reasons that emerge in favor of the legitimacy of this practice, including legal protection of the reproductive rights of the mother who still lives. In fact, the death of her husband or partner does not destroy the expectations that the

---

24 Lei 94-654, from July 29, 1994, regulating the use and donation of elements and parts of the human body, pre-natal diagnosis and medically assisted procreation.

25 Nathalie MASSAGER, *Les Droits de l'Enfant à Naitre*, p. 794 ss.

26 The Court of Palermo decided that the damage of growing up without a father cannot be compared to the damage of not being born (ruling from January 8, 1999). The same idea can be seen in the Italian Law (Law 40, of February 19, 2004, article 14/1), about assisted reproduction, which forbids the destruction of the embryos. This argument can lead to a great deal of discussions and raise some other relevant doubts, but this is not the adequate moment or place to bring them up.

woman had on those embryos nor her desire to be a mother, and may even strengthen it.

3. The solution under the Portuguese law

In Portugal this matter is regulated by article 22 of Law 32/2006 of 26 July. The epigraph of the act is called "post-mortem insemination," when strictly speaking it should be called "post-mortem embryo transfer," since only the latter practice is allowed, with everything else being forbidden (despite the fact that article 23 explains that any child born from a fertilization or post-mortem insemination – thereby circumventing the legal prohibition – will still be the son or daughter of the deceased).

In short, the Portuguese legislators defined the legal regime at the time of fertilization: should it occur before the death of the father allows the embryos to be transferred, but if it has not occurred by that date, it can no longer take place, even in spite of the evidences related to the wishes of the deceased. Nor is it expected that any document asking for a *post-mortem* fertilization will be considered valid by the courts.

All rules present on the Law 32/2006 assume that the one who dies is the male element, which suggests that *post mortem* transfer of embryos is always prohibited when it is the woman who dies, perhaps on the assumption that this procedure would require recourse to surrogacy. However, it is not necessarily so, since the biological father may want to use their embryos with his new partner.

However, this possibility raises some doubts, regarding to the respect for reproductive rights of women who died. But on the other hand, its prohibition does not imply, by way of congruence, in a concomitant ban on marrying a widower and his new wife adopted the children of previous marriage? That is, to what extent is that the embryo transfer made after the death of the biological mother affects to a greater extent the rights of the parallel situation in which their children are orphans adopted by her husband's new wife?

4. The solution in the light of Brazilian law

In the absence of a specific legislation, we must make decisions based on the interpretation of various existing elements in Brazilian law, whether constitutional or derived from other sources.

Historically, one of these sources, Resolution 1.358/92 of the Federal Council of Medicine, which established ethical standards for the use of assisted reproduction techniques, has recently been repealed and replaced by Resolution 1.957/10.

In its general principles, the revoked resolution emphasized the importance – and obligation – of informed consent to the adoption of any measures or treatments with reproductive purposes. By establishing specific standards for the cryopreservation of gametes or pre-embryos, which stated that "at the time of cryopreservation, spouses or partners should express their willingness in writing as to the destination that will be given to pre-embryos cryopreserved in the event of divorce, serious illness or death of one or both of them, and when they wish to donate them. "

Resolution 1.957/10, establishing new regulatory and ethical standards for the use of assisted reproduction techniques, do not skirt around the issue of *post mortem* assisted reproduction, setting in its item VIII that "*post mortem* assisted reproduction does not constitute an ethical fault if there is specific and prior authorization of the deceased for the use of cryopreserved biological material, in accordance with current legislation. "

From the ethical point of view, therefore, the question emerges to recognize the autonomy of the will of the couple, in respect to matters of family planning, with assisted reproduction, and providing for the use of these techniques even after the eventual death of a member of the couple.

The Federal Constitution, on the other hand establishes "special state protection" for the family in its article 226, and pontificates on its paragraph 7 that "Based on the principles of human dignity and responsible parenthood, family planning is a free choice of the couple, and the State shall provide educational and scientific resources to exercise this right, without any form of coercion by official or private institutions. "

The Brazilian Civil Code, in turn, faces the issue on its article 1597, by stating that:

> Article 1597. They are presumed to be conceived during the marriage the children:
> I – born one hundred eighty days, at least, after established the conjugal life;

> II – born three hundred days after the dissolution of marriage, death, legal separation, nullity and annulment of marriage;
> III – born through the use of homologous artificial fertilization, even though the husband is dead;
> IV – born at any time, in the case of excedentary embryos resulting from homologous artificial conception;
> V – born through the use of heterologous artificial insemination, provided the existence of prior permission from the husband.

Still, the question of inheritance remains.

There is an obvious conflict between the Brazilian Civil Code and the Federal Constitution. The Code, in its article 1798, states that "The persons born or conceived at the time of the opening of the succession are legitimate to succeed."

The following article adds that "In inheritance can still be called to succeed: the children not yet conceived of persons nominated by the testator, as long as they live at the opening of the succession."

It happens that with the advances already seen in assisted reproduction techniques, the birth of these children can be protracted in time, leaving, therefore, the testamentary law dissociated from reality.

Eduardo de Oliveira Leite argues that "a child born after the death of biological parents, by the use of frozen semen, is an anomalous situation, both in terms of affiliation, or succession rights. In this case the child does not inherit from his father because he was not conceived at the opening of succession".[27]

This position, however, should not prosper. You can not, on behalf of an alleged legal, trample constitutionally guaranteed rights, because of the ineptitude of the legislators to adapt the rules to the reality. Yet, when by virtue of the Civil Code, which establishes the possibility of action of heritage petition in its article 1824, one sees that the condition of being a heir is not lost, and is therefore imprescriptible.

With regard to inheritance and succession rights (a right that is constitutionally regarded as fundamental, and embodied in article 5, XXX of the Constitution), it should be noted that the Constitution

---

27 In *Comentários ao Novo Código Civil,* vol. XXI, p. 110.

also determines (Article 227, paragraph 6) that there is not how to establish different rules, or distinction between the children with regard to rights and qualifications. This is, by the way, the same orientation contained in article 1596[28] of the Brazilian Civil Code.

Thus, it is necessary in the light of new scientific techniques and possibilities, fill in the legislative void, establishing ways to ensure that these children may be generated after the death of a parent, reassuring the inheritance rights that the constitution grants them.

Finally, a comment on this. There are those who argue it is impossible to hold any inheritance to children conceived by assisted reproductive techniques *post mortem*, invoking the principle of legal security in relationships. Constitutionally, however, the issue is deeper. The main issue here is dignity, as stated in article 226 of the Constitution, mentioned earlier. Dignity of the person, which is not "just" a constitutional principle, but the foundation of the Republic, as set out in article 1, III, of the Federal Constitution.

This being the basis, take precedence over any principles that may be invoked, and legislation must conform to it, and not vice versa.

5. Critical considerations

It seems hat the case raises no greater obstacle to the admissibility of the *post mortem* reproduction, even in their way of insemination or fertilization, specially when the father has left a prior informed consent authorizing the procedure.[29]

In favor of this solution there are the following arguments:

> i) First of all, respect for the wishes of deceased persons who expressed this desire in life;

28 Article 1.596. "Os filhos, havidos ou não da relação de casamento, ou por adoção, terão os mesmos direitos e qualificações, proibidas quaisquer designações discriminatórias relativas à filiação".

29 In favor of *post mortem* reproduction, Mary WARNOCK, "Reproductive Technologies...", p 364 ("I, for one do not see anything intrinsically harmful or wrong in the birth of a posthumous child, and therefore see no moral objection, in general, to the taking of steps to enable such a child to be born").

ii) Then, the parallelism between the *post mortem* reproduction and cases of pregnancies that continue despite the death of parents. It is true that the analogy is not complete, since, in the case of a natural pregnancy, the child will be born, at the very limit, nine months after his father's death, while using *post mortem* reproduction techniques, the child could be born much later, and this delay time (which may continue for years) is likely to disrupt the family structure, not only in terms of affection, but also in issues such as property (inheritance law). Therefore we advocate that the process should be carried out within a delimited time frame. In any situation, however, it is necessary to draw up legislation to regulate the procedure, bringing stability and safety to the legal relationship.

It seems that the Portuguese legislators did well by allowing the embryo transfer, and they could do much better if they decide to follow Spain´s example, authorizing fertilization *post mortem* based on a consent document, as defined in the first part of article 2, section 2 of the Spanish law.[30]

We suggest that this should also be the option for the Brazilian legislators, creating objective conditions to respect and enforce the autonomy and the will of people who may have left genetic material to allow post mortem reproduction, adapting the legal rules to new times and behaviors, ensuring legal safety and social peace.

30 "No obstante lo dispuesto en el apartado anterior, el marido podrá prestar su consentimiento, en el documento a que se hace referencia en el artículo 6.3, en escritura pública, en testamento o documento de instrucciones previas, para que su material reproductor pueda ser utilizado en los 12 meses siguientes a su fallecimiento para fecundar a su mujer. Tal generación producirá los efectos legales que se derivan de la filiación matrimonial. El consentimiento para la aplicación de las técnicas en dichas circunstancias podrá ser revocado en cualquier momento anterior a la realización de aquéllas".
Mais dúvidas nos desperta a segunda parte da norma ao estipular: "Se presume otorgado el consentimiento a que se refiere el párrafo anterior cuando el cónyuge supérstite hubiera estado sometido a un proceso de reproducción asistida ya iniciado para la transferencia de preembriones constituidos con anterioridad al fallecimiento del marido".

References

ALMEIDA, José Luiz Gavião de. *Código Civil Comentado. Direitos das Sucessões. Sucessão em geral. Sucessão Legítima – vol. XVIII*. São Paulo: Atlas, 2003.

ANDORNO, Roberto; BILLER-ANDORNO, Nikola; BRAUER, Susanne – "Advance Health Care Directives: Towards a Coordinated European Policy?", *European Journal of Health Law*, Vol. 16, n.º 3, 2009

BERGÉ, Jean-Sylvestre – "Tourisme Procréatif et Droit Communautaire Européen des Echanges: Le Cas Blood", in *Biomedicine, the Family and Human Rights*, (eds. Marie-Thérèse Meulders-Klein, Ruth Deech, Paul Vlaardingerbroek), Kluwer Law International, The Hauge, London, New York, 2002

CAMPIGLIO, Cristina – *Procreazione Assistita e Famiglia nel Diritto Internazionale*, CEDAM, Padova, 2003

CARCABA FERNÁNDEZ, María – *Los Problemas Jurídicos Planteados por las Nuevas Técnicas de Procreación Humana*, J. M. Bosch Editor, S. A., Barcelona, 1995

DEECH, Ruth – "Losing Control? – Some Cases", in *Biomedicine, the Family and Human Rights*, (eds. Marie-Thérèse Meulders-Klein, Ruth Deech, Paul Vlaardingerbroek), Kluwer Law International, The Hauge, London, New York, 2002

FERRAZ Sérgio – *Manipulações Biológicos e Princípios Constitucionais: Uma Introdução*, Sérgio António Fabros Editor, Porto Alegre, 1991

HARRIS, John – "Rights and Reproductive Choice", in *The Future of Human Reproduction*, (John Harris and Soren Holm, eds.) Clarendon Press, Oxford, 1998

LEITE, Eduardo de Oliveira. *Comentários ao Novo Código Civil, vol. XXI: do direito das sucessões, 2ª Ed., Rio de Janeiro: Forense, 2003.*

LOBO, Paulo Luiz Neto. *Código Civil Comentado: Direito de Família. Relações de Parentesco. Direito Patrimonial – vol. XVI*. Álvaro Vilaça Azevedo (coordenador). São Paulo: Atlas, 2003.

LURGER, Brigitta – "Das Fortpflanzungsmedizingesetz vor dem österreichischen Verfassungsgerichtshof", *Deutsches und Europäisches Familienrecht*, Volume 2, Number 3 / August, 2000

MASON, J. K.; SMITH, R.A.; LAURIE, G. T. – *Law and Medical Ethics*, 6th ed., Butterworths, Lexis Nexis, London etc., 2002

MASSAGER, Nathalie – *Les Droits de l'Enfant à Naitre*, Colection de la Faculté de Droit de l'Université Libre de Bruxelles, Bruylant, Bruxelles, 1997

PEREIRA, André – *O Consentimento Informado na Relação Médico-Paciente*, Coimbra Editora, Coimbra, 2004

PEREIRA, André – "Advance Directives: Binding or Merely Indicative? Incoherence of the Portuguese National Council of Ethics for the Life Sciences and Insufficiencies of Newly Proposed Regulation", *European Journal of Health Law*, Vol. 16, n.º 2, 2009

QUEIROZ, Juliane Fernandes. *Paternidade: aspectos jurídicos e técnicas de inseminação artificial*. Belo Horizonte: Del Rey, 2001.

SÁNDOR, Judit – "Reproduction and Genetics: Pragmatic and Moral Elements in the Hungarian Biomedical Law", in *Yearbook of European Medical Law*, The Institute of Medical Law, Sweeden, 2005

SÁNDOR, Judit – "Reproductive Rights in the Hungarian Law: A New Right to Assisted Procreation?", *Health and Human Rights*, 4(2), 2000

SHENFIELD, Françoise – "Panorama de la Reproducción Assitida en el Reino Unido: Regulación y Afectos", in *Bioética 2000*, Ediciones Nobel, Oviedo, 2000

ZANELLATO, Marco António – "Fertilização Artificial: Efeitos Jurídicos", *Revista Portuguesa de Direito do Consumo*, n.º 36, 2003

WARNOCK, Mary – "Reproductive Technologies: The Ehics of Provision", in *Basic Ethical Principles in European Bioethics and Biolaw,*(Jacob Dahl RENDTORFF, Peter KEMP eds.), *Volume II, Autonomy, Dignity, Integrity and Vulnerability*, Centre for Ethics and Law, Copenhagen, Denmark / Institut Borja de Bioetica, Barcelona, Spain, 2000.

IV

The legal aspects of plastic surgery on foreign patients in Brazil

Eduardo Dantas

Medicine has been evolving in leaps, and the practical consequence for that is the changing of social behavior, the creation of new practices and the need to deal with dilemmas once only a product of science fiction creative authors. In Vitro Fertilization, cloning techniques, the manipulation of stem cells, genetic engineering, nanotechnology and the deciphering of the genoma code are just part of an almost endless list of medical advances that generated relevant noise in society´s behavior, creating issues that have to be dealt with by ethical and legal regulations.

Law and Medicine – two of the most ancient sciences known to mankind – have a historically troubled co-existence, with different views and concepts for the same facts. And these differences have grown even stronger in the last six decades, with the technological revolution that medicine has gone through.

And the law can only change when required – even provoked – by these social movements, to define new limits, limitations and rules. In other words, to provide solution to the newly created conflicts. And it takes time. All the way in between these two points of the journey, there is uncertainty, legal breaches, and conflict.

Not only Brazil, but the whole world is suffering from the effects of being right in the middle of these troubled times, where Law and Medicine struggle to define the new shape of the legal rules regulating healthcare. That´s exactly why Bioethics and Medical Law have become so prominent in the last few years.

Were it possible to determine when the discussion of medical law started to gain importance in the Brazilian legal system, the probable date would be the year of 1992, when the Consumer´s Defense Code

(CDC) was enacted and put into effect. Still today, Medicine is a profession that resents from the lack of a proper Federal Law, defining its rights and obligations, its boundaries and frontiers.

As a result, higher courts started using the concept of *consumer* and *service providers* as defined in the CDC, using those definitions to solve conflicts between patients and physicians. That still creates an almost tangible tension between the courts and medical associations, with these last ones rejecting the possibility of having the medical profession considered as a consumer-oriented relationship.

The recently enacted Medical Ethics Code (a resolution, not a law, issued by the Federal Council of Medicine) expressly excludes the possibility of considering the practice of medicine as an activity regulated by the CDC. On the other hand, courtroom decisions apply the CDC in the rulings and sentences.

Which brings us to our topic.

The so-called "Medical Tourism" is a modern phenomena. A new kind of tourism has been attracting foreigners to Brazil: plastic surgery and medical procedures. Lower costs, and a good reputation of Brazilian surgeons has helped to build a significant market share in the last two decades, that now – estimates say – answers for over 3% of all aesthetical procedures, in a business that performed more than 600.000 surgeries last year alone, in a growing movement that still haven´t found its boundaries.

Plastic surgery is just one – or the most visible – aspect of this new way of searching for medical treatment. Oncology, Dentistry, and Assisted Reproduction Techniques, to name a few, are some of the branches that benefits from globalization.

Although the impact in the economy is more than obvious – Thailand, India, and Malaysia, world leaders in medical tourism, profited more than one billion dollars in 2005 alone – some legal implications are still unknown. The legal system has still a long way to define clear rules – involving bioethics, international law, consumer law, criminal law and tort law, for instance – in order to bring safety to the new relationship being established between a physician and a foreign patient.

Four factors attract patients to perform medical interventions in Brazil: The first one is the cost. Compared to United States and some European countries, the amount of money necessary for a treatment can be very different, allowing a patient to pay not only for the treatment, but also for the air ticket, hotels, and even some real tourism. And still, one cannot forget that over 40 million north-americans do not have healthcare insurance and need to pay for their medical treatments, being a potential group for this business.

The second factor is prestige. Brazilian surgeons are renowned in the international medical community by their expertise, and the quality of their work, being plastic surgery, by far, the most popular one.

The third factor would be the doctor x patient relationship. Studies have shown that in Brazil, consultation takes more time, there´s more talk, and doctors are more open to understand what the patient wants. The relationship – yet – is not so cold, because medical malpractice issues haven´t started transforming the physician´s offices into a war theater.

And the fourth factor is that there are less restrictions in the Brazilian Medicine than in other countries, when it comes to the possibility of adopting new treatment or procedures. Doctors are more open to the possibility of being less conservative, backed by law.

In Italy, for instance, sperm donation, surrogate motherhood, and the freezing of embryos are forbidden. Artificial insemination is restricted to stable or married couples. The absence of such restriction attract attract Italian couples to cross the ocean to perform *in vitro* fertilization in Brazil.

In the U.S. doctors and dentists avoid certain procedures, by fear of being sued. Dental implant, for example, with a 15% rate of unexpected results, is a potential source of legal problems, and patients are referred to Brazilian dentists to perform the treatment. Brazilian Society of Aesthetical Odontology estimates that, last year alone, 2.500 people went to Brazil seeking for this kind of treatment.

This kind of medical business is becoming more and more interesting for the touristic trade, since these patients stay longer, and spend more than any other group of tourists.

But there is still a long way to go to become a leading player in this field. Just to present some numbers, The Bumrungrad Hospital, in Bangcok – Thailand, receives 350.000 foreign patients per year, having profited last year alone, over half a billion dollars with this.

Some key guidelines are recommended for travelers who seek medical treatment, and cannot be left unsaid, in order to create a safer environment for doctors and for patients, by helping to define duties, rights and responsibilities:

What is the surgeon's training?
A gynecologist performing a breast augmentation or a dermatologist doing a face lift are not appropriate choices.

Is the surgeon certified?
Ask for certification information and who the certifying body is.

Does the patient´s personal health insurance provides coverage outside the country?
Most health insurance providers do not cover individuals for surgery performed outside their own country. The patient has to consider obtaining International Medical Coverage that may be available through his insurance agent.

What about aftercare?
Patients should stay in the area where the surgery was performed for at least one week, depending on the procedure. The patient has to find out in advance where he will stay and if this facility is prepared to care for his post operative needs.

What about complications?
What doctor will care for the patient at home if he has complications and who will pay for secondary or revision procedures?

Do the key personnel at the surgeon's office speak your language fluently?
If the patient cannot be easily understood, be prepared for complications.

With whom are you communicating?
The patient should be talking directly with the doctor's staff and the doctor. A travel agent should only make travel and accommodations arrangements.

Is the surgeon a member of recognized national and international societies?

As to legal issues, being under the protection of the Consumer´s Defense Code, a foreign patient can sue the doctor in case of malpractice. There are, though, complications. Even with the possibility of doing that at his home country, the patient would have to deal with international laws, and submit his plea under Brazilian laws and parameters. Probably the best way to do it would be filing the complaint in Brazilian territory, but the legal costs of the process, and the time required to solve the demand would be a barrier to do so.

Up to now, higher courts did not have to face such demands, but with the growing numbers of procedures, it may just be a matter of time. And when it happens, new guidelines may be necessary to help solve problems created by this new, modern way of practicing medicine in a world without physical barriers, but with very present legal frontiers.

V

Informed Choice: Building the bridge between Informed Consent and Autonomy

Eduardo Dantas

Abstract: The so-called informed consent, as conventionally understood, is not synonymous with valid consent, because it´s just part of the process of enabling and respecting patient´s autonomy. Consenting is just a part of the process of choosing, and is not enough to allow patients to exercise their right to autonomy. This can only be accomplished through the complete and understandable disclosure of all information regarding treatment, their options and possible consequences.

Keywords: Informed consent. Informed choice. Right to information. Informational negligence. Autonomy.

1. Introduction

The history of medicine established its foundations on the notion that the determining factor of the relationship with the patient was the superiority of the physician´s view and knowledge, granting him powers over the patient, including those of deciding what was better for this last one, even against (and most of the times ignoring) the patient´s moral codes, beliefs and value systems.[1]

1 "Paternalism centres on the notion that the physician... has better insight into the best interests of the patient than does the patient, or that the physician´s obligations are such that he is impelled to do what is medically good, even if it

The last six decades changed our views on the relationship between a physician and his patients. The paternalistic component lost most of its importance (and in some cases, its almost divine aspect), and autonomy began to be seen as a key element for treatment and research using human subjects.

One of the most important modern documents that provided philosophical foundations for the moral justification of this shift in medical ethics was the *Belmont Report*, published in 1979 by the North American National Comission for the Protection of Human Subjects of Biomedical and Behavioral Research, as a response to the debates generated after some landmark cases, such as Nuremberg and Tuskegee, discussed below.

Among other issues, the Report stated that "to respect autonomy is to give weight to autonomous persons´ considered opinions and choices while refraining from obstructing their actions unless they are clearly detrimental to others. To show lack of respect for an autonomous agente is to repudiate that person´s considered judgments, to deny an individual the freedom to act on those considered judgments, or to withhold information necessary to make a considered judgment, when there are no compelling reasons to do so".

When one speaks about the right to information in the healthcare context, there is an almost automatic association to the expression "informed consent". It is virtually unanimous nowadays in modern society the idea that every medical intervention or experiment must be previously understood and consented by the patient or subject of research, in order to prevent liability.

It wasn´t always like this. To a better understanding of the present situation, it is important to look at it with a historic perspective. The first centuries of medicine were defined by a dichotomy of presumed superiority between the guardians of the medical knowledge, and the patients. The art of medicine was seen as something divine, almost supernatural, and little or no questioning was allowed regarding the decisions and commands issued by those few men of science.

---

is not ´good´ in terms of the patient´s own value system". E.D. Pelligrino and D.C. Thomasma, *For the patient´s good* (New York: Oxford University Press, 1988), p. 7.

The concept that the patient – as a human being – was entitled to certain rights, began to grow after the French Revolution, and later, after the Industrial Revolution. The physicians were slowly stripped of their divine origin, being regarded as a normal citizen, an ordinary professional, subject thus to failure and questioning.

Philosophers like Immanuel Kant *(Foundations of the Metaphysics of Morals) and* John Stuart Mill *(On Liberty)* developed the idea of respect for autonomy, recognizing, through the Kantian notion of *categorical imperatives* that autonomy was inherent to the human condition, thus forcing society to prevent treating patients as means to an end, since their individuality was an end in itself.

Mill[2] even stated that "the only purpose for which power can be rightfully exercised over any member of a civilised community, against his will, is to prevent harm to others. His own good, either physical or moral, is not a sufficient warrant... Over himself, over his own body and mind the individual is sovereign".

Not by chance, the second half of the eighteenth century saw the first statement coming from a legal decision, in the famous *Slater v Baker and Stapleton*[3] case, in which the doctors were found guilty of performing treatment, refracturing the patient´s legs, without his previous knowledge and consent.

At the same time, and for several reasons, in the subsequent years medical services began to lose the personal touch, surrendering to the market and the image of the doctor became something distant and unknown to the patient, raising legal issues about criminal, civil, and ethical responsibility, establishing the grounds for the informed consent doctrine in the patient-doctor relationship.

---

2 *On Liberty*, ed. Gertrude Himmelfarb (Harmondsworth: Penguin, 1974), p. 71. *Apud* SALAKO, Solomon. "Informed consent under the European Convention on Biomedicine and the Unesco Declaration on Bioethics", *in Medicine and Law,* n. 30, vol. 01, Haifa: Probook, pp. 101-113, jan/2011.

3 (1967) 2 Wils KB359, 95 ER 860.

2. Bioethics and the legal development of the principle of patient´s autonomy

Since the end of World War II, the bioethical concept of patient autonomy[4] has gained importanc,[5] shifting the centuries-old balance in the paternalistic relation between physicians and their patients.[6]

Of course, case law stating the importance of consent can be found in the anglo-saxonic jurisprudence since the late years of the 18th

---

4 "Autonomy is a form of personal liberty of action where the individual determines his or her own course of action in accordance with a plan chosen by himself or herself. The autonomous person is one who not only deliberates about and chooses such plans but who is capable of acting on the basis of such deliberations, just as a truly independent government has autonomous control of its territories and policies." Beauchamp, T. & Childress, J. *Principles of biomedical ethics*. New York: Oxford University Press, 1979, pp. 56-57.

5 "Respect for autonomy is the most frequently mentioned moral principle in the literature on informed consent, where it is conceived as a principle rooted in the liberal Western tradition of the importance of individual freedom of choice, both for political life and for personal development. ´Autonomy´ and ´respect for autonomy´ are terms loosely associated with several ideas, such as privacy, voluntariness, self-mastery, choosing freely, the freedom to choose, choosing one´s own moral position, and accepting responsibilities for one´s choices.". Beauchamp, T. & Faden, R. A *history and theory of informed consent*. New York: Oxford University Press, 1986, p. 7.

6 "Part of the explanation for the shift from beneficent paternalism toward autonomy lies in historical events of the twentieth century, primarily related to research, that called into question the trustworthiness of the medical profession. The atrocities revealed in the Nuremberg Trial of Nazi doctors, as well as highly publicized cases of human subjects abused in the United States, sparked suspicion of the general benevolence of physicians and researchers. In this context, informed consent was seen as a protection from abuse by untrustworthy professionals. Even if the medical and research establishment could not be trusted to conduct prospective review of the likely harms and benefits and to offer individuals only research and treatment opportunities that had acceptable risk-benefit ratios, individuals could safeguard their own interests if they were adequately informed and if their autonomous authorization was required before research or treatment could proceed. Individuals were thus called upon to exercise their autonomous decisional authority to safeguard their welfare". BERG, Jessica W. [Et Al], Informed Consent, 2nd ed, Oxford University Press, New York, 2001, p. 20.

Century,[7] but it was only after the Nuremberg trials,[8-9] and moreover, the Tuskegee´s experiments,[10] that informed consent became one of

7 Slater *v.* Baker and Stapleton, 2 Wils. K.B. 358 (1767). In this case, the plaintiff hired the defendants to remove the bandages from his fractured leg. Against the patient´s will and in spit of his protests, both physicians decided to refracture the plaintiff´s leg and place it in an experimental device to stretch and straighten it during rehealing. In the reasoning, the Court stated: "In answer to this, it appears from the evidence of the surgeons that it was improper to disunite the callous [bony material in healing] without consent; this is the usage and law of surgeons: then it was ignorance and unskillfulness in that very particular, to do contrary to the rule of the profession, what no surgeon ought to have done; and indeed it is reasonable that a patient should be told what is about to be done to him, that he may courage and put himself in such a situation as to enable him to undergo the operation".

8 For more detailed information, it is recommended reading Norbert Ehrenfreund´s "The Nuremberg Legacy: How the Nazi War Crimes Trials changed the course of history" (2007, Palgrave Macmillan); Robert E. Conot´s "Justice at Nuremberg" (1993, Basic Books); and Michael R. Marrus´ "The Nuremberg War Crimes Trial, 1945-46: A documentary history"(1997, Bedford/ St. Martin´s).

9 The Nuremberg Code (http://www.cirp.org/library/ethics/nuremberg/) states in its article first that "The voluntary consent of the human subject is absolutely essential. This means that the person involved should have legal capacity to give consent; should be so situated as to be able to exercise free power of choice, without the intervention of any element of force, fraud, deceit, duress, overreaching, or other ulterior form of constraint or coercion; and should have sufficient knowledge and comprehension of the elements of the subject matter involved as to enable him to make an understanding and enlightened decision. This latter element requires that before the acceptance of an affirmative decision by the experimental subject there should be made known to him the nature, duration, and purpose of the experiment; the method and means by which it is to be conducted; all inconveniences and hazards reasonably to be expected; and the effects upon his health or person which may possibly come from his participation in the experiment. The duty and responsibility for ascertaining the quality of the consent rests upon each individual who initiates, directs, or engages in the experiment. It is a personal duty and responsibility which may not be delegated to another with impunity."

10 Again, for more information, it is recommended reading Susan M. Reverby´s "Examining Tuskegee: The infamous Syphilis Study and its legacy" (2009, The University of North Carolina Press), with an analysis of the notorious study of untreated syphilis, which took place in and around Tuskegee, Alabama, from the 1930s through the 1970s. The study involved hundreds of African Ameri-

the pillars of modern medicine, and almost the Holy Grail of medical ethics.

The foundations of this doctrine can be found mostly in the North-American case law jurisprudence, though. In 1905, the leading case Mohr vs. Williams[11] raised the issue wheter the patient gives a physician specific consent to operate, does the physician have general consent to perform other surgical operations undertaken to treat other problems? In this case, the patient arranged for the physician, an ear specialist, to perform surgery on her right ear After Williams began performing the operation he decided that Mohr's left ear rather than her right ear required surgery, although the condition was not life threatening. Williams operated successfully on the left ear without having received permission from Mohr.

Mohr sued Williams for battery and the court decided that when a doctor obtains a patient's specific consent for a particular operation he may not perform another operation on the patient without her consent. A patient's consent is implied when an emergency situation arises. However, this does not allow the doctor a free license to attempt to remedy all problems found that are not life threatening. The court held that in this case, there was no evidence that the condition of the plaintiff's left ear presented a serious or life threatening situation.

Even though there was no showing that he had a wrongful intent or that he had been negligent, Williams was still liable for battery.[12] The court held that it was not relevant that the operation was successful.

The same understanding was reinforced in 1914 in the United States, during the leading case of *Schoendorff v. Society of New York Hospitals,*[13] discussing a situation where the patient had undergone surgical intervention without his previous consent. The New York

can men, most of whom were told by the doctors from the U.S. Public Health Service that they were being treated, not just watched, for their late-stage syphilis; and from the same author, "Tuskegee´s truths: Rethinking the Tuskegee Syphilis study" (2000, The University of North Carolina Press).

11 1905, Mohr *v.* Williams, 104 N.W. 12

12 "The free citizen's first and great right – the right to himself .... this right necessarily forbids a physician .... to violate without permission the bodily integrity of his patient"

13 Schoendorff v. Society of New York Hospital, 106 N.E. 93 (N.Y. 1914)

Court held accountable the hospital for violating the patient´s body integrity, in spite of the positive outcome. Justice Benjamin Cardozo stated in his ruling that "every human being of adult years and sound mind has a right to determine what shall be done with his own body", words that became paramount for the informed consent doctrine with the passing of the years.

The expression "informed consent" appeared for the first time in 1957, in the leading case Salgo *vs.* Leland Stanford Junior University Board of Trustees,[14] dealing with a malpractice case where the patient found himself paralyzed in his lower members after a surgical procedure, without being informed of such possibility as a risk. The case decided that proper consent required provision of information. In the ruling, the judges decided that the physician has the duty to **disclose *"any* facts** *which are necessary to form the basis of an intelligent consent by the patient to the proposed treatment*".

In the French doctrine, one of the first trials regarding patient´s rights happened in 1942, and not by chance deals with consent issues.[15] The concept of *consentement éclairé* is widely spread in France, present in several laws, like the Law from December 20th 1978 (regulating biomedical experiences), the Law 94.653 from July 29th 1994 (inserting article 16, section 3[16] in the French Civil Code), and the 1995´s French Medical Ethics Code, reinforcing the evidence and necessity of respecting the informed consent doctrine.

14 Salgo *v.* Leland Stanford Jr. University Board of Trustees, 317 P.2d. 170 (Cal. App. 1957)

15 Cf. André Pereira, *in* O consentimento informado na relação médico-paciente, Ed. Coimbra, Coimbra, 2004, p. 61: *Cour Cassation*, 28-1-1942 *(arrêt* Teyssier): "... attendu que, comme tout chirurgien, le chirurgien d'um service hospitalier est tenu, sauf cas de force majeure, d'obtenir le consentement du malade avant de pratiquer une opération dont il apprécie, en pleine independence, sous la responsabilité, l'utilité, la nature et les risques; qu'en violant cette obligation, imposéé par le respect de la personne humaine, il commet une atteinte grave aux droits du malade, un manquement à sés devoir proprement médicaux et qui constitue une faute personelle se détachant de l'exercice de sés fonctions...".

16 Code Civil, art. 16, n. 3: "Il ne peu être porté atteinte à l'integrité du corps humain qu'en cas de necessite médicale pour la personne. Le consentement de l'interessé doit être recueilli préalablement dans le cas ou son état rend nécessai-re une intervention thérapeutique à laquelle il n'est pas à même de consentir".

In 1973, The American Hospitals Association were the first to implement the Patient's Bill of Rights which specified the right of any patient to receive complete and comprehensive medical information that he can evaluate and understand. The patient was given the right to accept or to refuse the recommended treatment after being advised of the consequences of his decision: "The patient has the right to obtain from the physician **complete current information** concerning his diagnosis, treatment and prognosis in terms the patient can reasonably expected to **understand.** The patient has the right to receive from his physician information necessary to give **informed consent** prior to start of any procedure and/or treatment.[17] The patient has the right to **refuse** treatment to the extent permitted by law, and to be informed of the medical consequences of his action."

Another North-American leading case followed in the same direction. *Canterbury vs. Spence,*[18] from 1972. Its historical relevance lies on the demonstration of the imperative necessity of the patient´s understanding of the information transmitted by the doctor before a surgical intervention. In this case, the patient, who developed a paralysis after a laminectomy hasn´t been informed of a 1% risk possibility of occurring such side effect. The Court ruled that:

> "A physician is under a duty to treat his patient skillfully but proficiency in diagnosis and therapy is not the full measure of his responsibility. The cases demonstrate that the physician is under an obligation to communicate specific information to the patient when the exigencies of reasonable care call for it. Due care may require a physician perceiving symptoms of bodily abnormality to alert the patient to the condition. It may call upon the

17 A physician should convey the risks of an operation when a reasonable person would be likely to attach significance to the risk in deciding whether or not to forgo the proposed therapy. The standard measuring performance of the duty to disclose is conduct which is reasonable under the circumstances. There are two exceptions to this general rule: (1) where the patient is unconscious and harm from a failure to treat is greater than any harm threatened by the proposed treatment; and (2) where disclosing the risk to the patient poses a threat to the patient´s well being.

18 Canterbury v Spence, 464 F.2d 772 (DC Cir 1972)

physician confronting an ailment which does not respond to his ministrations to inform the patient thereof. It may command the physician to instruct the patient as to any limitations to be presently observed for his own welfare, and as to any precautionary therapy he should seek in the future. It may oblige the physician to advise the patient of the need for or desirability of any alternative treatment promising greater benefit than that being pursued. Just as plainly, due care normally demands that the physician warn the patient of any risks to his well-being which contemplated therapy may involve.

(...)

In our view, the patient's right of self-decision shapes the boundaries of the duty to reveal. That right can be effectively exercised only if the patient possesses enough information to enable an intelligent choice. The scope of the physician's communications to the patient, then, must be measured by the patient's need, and that need is the information material to the decision. Thus the test for determining whether a particular peril must be divulged is its materiality to the patient's decision: all risks potentially affecting the decision must be unmasked. And to safeguard the patient's interest in achieving his own determination on treatment, the law must itself set the standard for adequate disclosure.

(...)

The topics importantly demanding a communication of information are the inherent and potential hazards of the proposed treatment, the alternatives to that treatment, if any, and the results likely if the patient remains untreated. The factors contributing significance to the dangerousness of a medical technique are, of course, the incidence of injury and the degree of the harm threatened. A very small chance of death or serious disablement may well be significant; a potential disability which dramatically outweighs the potential benefit of the therapy or the detriments of the existing malady may summons discussion with the patient."

In 1989, deciding a case in the UK courts,[19] Lord Donaldson MR stated in his ruling that:

> "The ability of the ordinary adult to exercise a free choice in deciding whether to accept or refuse medical treatment and to choose between treatments is not to be dismissed as desirable but inessential. It is a crucial factor in relation to all medical treatment".

3. Informed Consent, the duty to inform and informed choice

There are several legal issues regarding consent,[20] and litigation is increasing in relation to consent issues. Too many aspects need to be taken into consideration for consent to be considered valid, such as when consent was obtained and whether the risks have been explained; moreover, whether they were understood by the patient (sometimes, cultural issues or language barriers can be a complication); whether the patient is a minor (if so, mature or not to decide by him/herself); whether an adult patient has legal capacity to decide (and also, if having legal capacity to decide, clinical capacity is absent); whether an oral consent constitutes enough evidence that information has been given and understood.

But above all – and that´s precisely the object of this study – whether the patients have been given sufficient, adequate, complete

---

19 *In Re F (Mental Patient: Sterilisation) (1990) 2 AC 1.*

20 Neil C. Manson and Onora O´Neill, in *Rethinking informed consent in bioethics* (New York: Cambridge University Press, 2007, p. 4) states that "contemporary discussions insist that informed consente should play a wider role in biomedicine than it was envisaged at the time of the Nuremberg Code. Informed consent requirements have been extended from research to clinical ethics, and standards for seeking and giving informed consent have been made more explicit and more demanding. The justifications given for requiring informed consent have supposedly been strenghtened by appeals to various conceptions of autonomy. Finally, informed consent requirements have been extended from medical treatment and research to the secondary use of information and tissues, by incorporating them into the regulation governing data protection, uses of human tissues and genetic technologies."

information, so that they can actually decide, and not just consent to a physician´s suggestion.

Very often, tough, physicians and health care providers misunderstand the concept of the so-called *informed consent.*[21]

Informed consent is the authorization given by the patient to undergo treatment, based on the knowledge of the nature of a medical procedure, and be submitted to risks, side effects, possible complications, benefits and alternatives to the proposed treatment. In other words, it is the acceptance of the services to be delivered by a healthcare professional, after understanding what is being consented to.

Manson and O´Neill[22] divide consent into two different categories: implicit and implied, or specific and generic:

> "The distinction between *explicit* and *implied* consent contrasts ways of consenting. Explicit consenting is a two way process. Those who request consent must provide an explicit statement of the nature and purposes of a proposed course of action, its effects, risks and other features, to those whose consent is sought. Those who are asked to consent must show explicitly that they understand this information and agree to the proposal. Explicit consenting os typically done using documents, signatures and formal statements, and in some cases witnesses who confirm and provide evidence that proper procedures for consenting have been followed.
>
> (...)
>
> The distinction between *specific* and *generic* consent applies not to acts of consenting, but to the propositions to which consent is given. The longer and more elaborate ´consent forms´ now routinely used in the NHS, and in medical

21 "It is always an open question whether an autonomous person with the capacity to give an informed consent actually has, in any specific instance, given an informed consent, in the sense of making an autonomous choice to authorize or refuse an intervention". Faden, R, Beauchamp, T L, A *History and theory of informed consent,* Oxford University Press, 1986, p. 237.

22 Neil C. Manson, Onora O´Neill, *Rethinking Informed Consent in Bioethics*, Cambridge University Press, 2007, pp. 10-11.

practice elsewhere, extend demands for (more) specific consent into the routine procedures of hospitals, the daily life of physicians and the daily experience of patients. These demands are seen as raising ethical standards for clinical practice by sharpening up not only processes of consenting, but the specificity of consent given."

It is necessary to understand that the process of consenting constitutes, at the same time, a patient´s right and a physician´s duty[23]. The patient must be informed in a clear and comprehensible way, according to his cognitive capabilities, about his diagnostic, risks, prognosis, and existing treatment alternatives, even those the doctor do not think fit for the specific case.

It is also important to point out that the mere act of reading and signing a paper, a consent form, is not enough to release the physician from his duties, from his obligation to inform accordingly (even if this written form is an important piece of evidence of due diligence).

The right to be informed has nothing, or very little, to do with the true exercise of patient´s autonomy. The act of consenting *to* some treatment, research, experiment or surgical procedure is just part of a bigger process, where the patient can exercise its autonomy. Someone

---

23 Regarding this, see for example articles 22, 24, 26, 31 and 34 of the Brazilian Medical Ethics Code, issued by the Federal Council of Medicine as Resolution 1931/2009: "Art. 22 – [É vedado ao médico] Deixar de obter o consentimento do paciente ou de seu representante legal após esclarecê-lo sobre o procedimento a ser realizado, salvo em caso de risco iminente de morte"; "Art. 24 – [É vedado ao médico] Deixar de garantir ao paciente o exercício do direito de decidir livremente sobre sua pessoa ou seu bem-estar, bem como exercer sua autoridade para limitá-lo"; "Art. 26 – [É vedado ao médico] Deixar de respeitar a vontade de qualquer pessoa, considerada capaz fisica e mentalmente, em greve de fome, ou alimentá-la compulsoriamente, devendo cientificá-la das prováveis complicações do jejum prolongado e, na hipótese de risco iminente de morte, tratá-la"; "Art. 31 – [É vedado ao médico] Desrespeitar o direito do paciente ou de seu representante legal de decidir livremente sobre a execução de práticas diagnósticas ou terapêuticas, salvo em caso de risco iminente de morte"; "Art. 34 – [É vedado ao médico] Deixar de informar ao paciente o diagnóstico ou prognóstico, os riscos e os objetivos do tratamento, salvo quando a comunicação direta possa lhe provocar dano, devendo, nesse caso, fazer a comunicação a seu representante legal".

can consent (in the sense of agreement or assent), based on the trust put over the doctor, based on indifference, fear, or even *because* it didn´t receive all necessary information to really *choose* among different possible options.

Informed consent is often mistaken by informed choice – this last one being essential to achieve the fulfillment of the right to be informed (and the physician´s duty to inform).

The patient needs not only receive, but also understand the information that has been handed over, and not just simply receive it without processing it properly. Information without comprehension is legally void, because it could be proven that the patient consented (or signed a consent form), but did not exercise his right to free and informed choice. His autonomy would be jeopardized.

4. Autonomy and Consent to Medical Treatment under the European Convention on Human Rights and Biomedicine

Recognizing the need to establish boundaries to the evolution of biomedicine, and to create standard concepts for the protection of human beings in the field of health and biomedical research, the member States of the Council of Europe issued a declaration, definining rights and responsibilities to safeguard fundamental rights and freedoms of the individual. Among those rights, were the protection of autonomy, and those patiens not able to consent.

Article 5 of the Oviedo Convention (European Convention of Human Rights and Biomedicine, 1997), clearly provides that "*An intervention in the health field may only be carried out after the person concerned has given free and informed consent. This person shall beforehand be given appropriate information as to the purpose and nature of the intervention as well as on its consequence and risks. The person concerned may freely withdraw at any time.*"

Very similar to that, and just a few years later, UNESCO´s Universal Declaration on Biomedicine and Human Rights (2005) recognized the same principle of respect for autonomy, also in its article 5: "*The autonomy of persons to make decisions, while taking responsibility for those decisions and respecting the autonomy of others, is to be respected*".

And what can be considered appropriate information? That is a difficult question, since the answer may differ, given the specific situation. But mostly, the communication between the health care provider and his patient must include the existing treatment options (not only the main options) with their purposes and details, their benefits and risks (commonly occurring risks and those unlikely to occur), possible side-effects, success rates, the reasons why an specific option is being recommended, the prognosis, and the risks of not having treatment. In other words, the information disclosure has to be relevant and reasonable enough to make sure that the exercise of patient´s autonomy is effective and meaningful.

That being said, the act of obtaining consent without allowing proper choice doesn´t represent an automatic release from professional duties regarding information, if this was withheld, distorted, tampered with, or incomplete. The physician would still be held liable for informational negligence[24].

We have been stressing the importance of consent – and consent forms – over the past years, forgetting that there are more important situations to be dealt with, arising from the relationship in question. Let´s take as an example, article 5 of the European Convention on Human Rights and Biomedicine (the Oviedo Convention), as previously stated here. All attention is drawn to the first part of the text, which says that "*an intervention in the health field may only be carried out after the person concerned has given free and informed consent to it*". However, the key to understand the true spirit of the law lies in the second part of the article, which states that "*this person shall*

24 Regarding informational negligence, France had a particular prolific year in 2010, with important decisions issued by the *Cour de Cassation* recognizing civil responsibility and negligence for the breach of duty to inform the patient properly. For an overview of the French jurisprudence, it is recommended reading the decisions from January 28th, June 3rd and October 14th.
In Brazil, the Superior Court of Justice (STJ) also decided in favor of the plaintiff, helding a blood bank liable for lack of proper communication of test results (REsp nº 1.071.969/PE). In 2007, another case, involving plastic surgery (AgRg in Ag 818.144/SP) had a similar result, with the court ruling that "the physician who do not inform his patient about the risks of surgery is negligent, being liable for all damages resulting from the intervention". In the opposite direction, a case judged in 2009 (REsp 1.051.674/RS) exempted the doctor from being considered responsible for an unexpected result, because he proved the fulfillment of the duty to inform. All three rulings avaiable at www.stj.jus.br.

beforehand be given appropriate information as to the purpose and nature of the intervention as well as on its consequences and risks".

Again, UNESCO´s Universal Declaration on Biomedicine and Human Rights imposes the same need for information disclosure in its article 6, which states that "*Any preventive, diagnostic and therapeutic medical intervention is only to be carried out with the prior, free and informed consent of the person concerned, based on adequate information. The consent should where appropriate, be express and may be withdrawn by the person concerned at any time and for any reason without disadvantage or prejudice*".

In the same direction, Sheila McLean[25] highlights the importance of information in the process of consenting and choosing:

> "One way, it seems obvious, that we can facilitate the making of a valid choice, is by ensuring that the patient is provided with the wherewithal to make a decision in the first place. In other words, the patient needs information on which to base his or her choice. The "informed", or more accurately informational, aspect of consent is the element that focuses on the patient´s right to receive relevant and sufficient information in order to enable him or her to make a decision. It is generally assumed, then, that – in the absence of a competent refusal to receive any information that might be offered – a valid consent (or refusal) depends on the sharing of information with the patient. The doctor is, therefore, under an obligation to share information with his or her patient."

Appropriate information seems to be the main element about patient´s autonomy rights. The information, to be "appropriate", does NOT need to meet the doctor´s assessment of the situation, but the patient´s. All relevant data, alternatives (even those the physician thinks are not recommended to the case, based on its experience) and risks must be disclosed to the patient, in an understandable way, in

25 McLean, Sheila A. M., *Autonomy, Consent and the Law*, Routledge-Cavendish, 2010, p. 42

order to provide sufficient elements for a decision – a choice – to be made. This – and not consenting – is the real exercise of autonomy. These exact same ideas are exposed in article 5[26] of the Inter American Convention of Human Rights (1969).

As a matter of comparative law, in the U.S., the *Patient Self-determination Act* (1991) regulates the idea of the right to information as a basic requirement, being the right to informed consent just a part of the process, not its final goal. A consent form signed by the patient is not a safeguard from lawsuits. Of course, it´s an important document, but cannot be seen as the only thing that matters in defensive medicine.

The examples of legal documents could go on and on, in Brazil,[27] Portugal,[28] Spain,[29] France[30] and Israel,[31] and all over the world, showing that there is a new way of dealing with old dilemmas, and that health care providers have to adapt their concepts to the new ideas. The world has evolved, and that requires adaptation.

A patient doesn´t need to consent to a proposed treatment. This may come as a shock to many doctors, as they are trained to "fight" diseases, and save lives, no matter what. What they´re not taught in med schools is the fact that their main obligations – apart from acting with the best of their techniques and skills – is that they must provide information to the patient. The patient will decide, based on its personal life, values, morals and beliefs, which is the best option.

---

26 Article 5. Right to Humane Treatment – 1.Every person has the right to have his physical, mental, and moral integrity respected.

27 In Brazil, Federal laws, such as Law 8.080/1990 (Consumer´s Defense Code) article 7, section V, reinforces to the patient the right to information about his/her health conditions; Law 10.741/2003 (Elderly´s Protection Act) ensures the right to choose the most favourable health treatment; Law 9.434/1997 (Organ and Tissues Transplantation) requires consent for every procedure. State Law salso regulates patient´s rights, such as Law 10.204/1999 (São Paulo); Law 14.254/2003 (Paraná); and Law 16.279/2006 (Minas Gerais).

28 Deontological Code from the Portuguese Order of Physicians (Regulamento 14/2009), specially articles 44 to 51.

29 Ley 41/2002

30 Law of March 4th, 2002. And also, for example, article 1111-2 of the Public Health Code.

31 The Patient´s Rights Law, 1996.

Only then autonomy can be respected and enforced. These ideas are well explained in the words of Irene Switankowsky:[32]

> "The ultimate purpose of informed consent is to ensure that the patient makes an autonomous, rational, reflective, well-understood decision about a medical procedure or treatment alternative that s(he) believes will be most beneficial. In short, the ultimate purpose of properly informed consent is to protect a patient´s autonomy under all medical circumstances".

It is a mistake to think that obtaining informed consent – as it happens today in most of the cases – is enough to exempt the physician from liability, excluding legal responsibilities in the event of occurring an undesired outcome during the treatment or procedure.

A treatment or procedure can be considered successful from a clinical point of view, but later seen as inappropriate when confronted with other possible outcomes that could be expected if a different therapeutic method had been informed to – and chosen by – the patient.

This lack of information doesn´t necessarily means negligence. It may represent the expression of the physicians beliefs, based in his own experience or in the medical literature, that the proposed solution was the most adequate to the situation faced at a given moment. The problem is that this behavior goes against ethical principles and legal commands that consider mandatory the disclosure of all information available. Withholding information about alternatives may be considered – in a lawsuit or in a disciplinary investigation – an undue interference in treatment, thus breaching confidence and contrary to the principles of good-faith and autonomy.

This notion is no different in several jurisdictions. In fact, it represents a tendency towards autonomy, as can be seen in the words of André Pereira[33], when stating that "recently, some authors

---

32 Switankowsky, Irene S., A *new paradigm for informed consent*, University Press of America, 1998, p. 2

33 Pereira, André, *O consentimento informado na relação médico-paciente*, Ed. Coimbra, Coimbra, 2004, p. 74.

have been proposing a more comprehensive concept. The expression *informed consent* has been criticized in the anglo-saxonic doctrine, since information is but an aspect of proper consent (´comprehensive or enlightened consent´). Thus, the use of the expression *informed choice* is being suggested. This concept could comprise, among other aspects, information about the consequences of refusal or withdrawing consent, therapeutic alternatives, choice of medicinal products (implicating changes in the regulatory frame of advertisement, choice of medical facilities, etc.).

In the Portuguese law, it is well established the right to "information on the existing health services" and the "right to free choice of physician", and also the right to a "second opinion". All these aspects considered, they go beyond simple informed consent; they are advanced expressions of the right to an informed consent, in the modern version of *informed choice*: self-determination in health care implies not only patient´s consent or refusal to a proposed intervention, but in possessing all elements to analyze treatment possibilities in medical, chirurgical and pharmaceutical field"[34].

34 Translated from the original "Mais recentemente, alguns autores vêm propondo um conceito mais abrangente. Assim, na doutrina anglo-saxônica critica-se a expressão *informed consent*, visto que a informação é apenas um aspecto do consentimento esclarecido ("*comprehensive or enlightened consent*"). Assim, vem sendo proposta a utilização da expressão *informed choice*. Este conceito teria a virtude de abranger, entre outros aspectos, a informação sobre as conseqüências da recusa ou revogação do consentimento, as alternativas terapêuticas, a escolha dos medicamentos (o que implica alterações à regulamentação da publicidade dos medicamentos, a escolha do estabelecimento de saúde, etc.). No direito português encontramos consagrado o direito à "*informação sobre os serviços de saúde existentes*" e o "*direito à livre escolha do médico*", e ainda o direito à "*segunda opinião*". Tudo aspectos que vão para além do simples consentimento livre e esclarecido. São expressões avançadas do direito ao consentimento informado, na sua vertente mais moderna de *informed choice*: a autodeterminação nos cuidados de saúde implica, não só que o paciente consinta ou recuse uma (heteronomamente) determinada intervenção, mas que tenha todos elementos de análise sobre as possibilidades de tratamento possíveis, no domínio médico, cirúrgico e farmacêutico.".

The right to consent, as an attribute of personal autonomy, is fundamental to ethical medicine. Its components are: information disclosure, voluntariness, and competency. Breach of informed consent may be actionable as battery or as malpractice.

In other words, obtaining a so-called valid and regular informed consent may be considered void, if it is not a result of an informed choice, leaving the doctor vulnerable to the legal risks and to the unpredictability of the medical activity.

5. Closing remarks

> "To violate a person´s autonomy is to treat that person merely as a means, that is, in accordance with others´ goals without regard to that person´s own goals. Such treatment is a fundamental moral violation because autonomous persons are ends in themselves capable of determining their destinies."
>
> Beauchamp and Childress, *Principles of Biomedical Ethics*, 1994, 4th ed., p. 125.

Health care providers tend to think that the sanctity of life is the most important guarantee, and the most important fundamental right in modern constitutions in the western world. It´s *not*. Legislators – and philosophers – all over the world begin to understand *Human Dignity* as a fundamental principle. And that dying with dignity – choosing not to undergo painful treatments to prolong life beyond cure; choosing to withdraw useless treatment, leave the hospital and die at home, surrounded by family and friends instead of doctors, nurses and bipping machines; and even refusing treatments that would oppose deeply against a patient´s religious beliefs – is part of living with dignity. This is the fundamental right that must be enforced.

The physician´s obligation, then, is to help the patient in choosing what is best for him/her, providing complete and adequate information. Is the doctor more prepared to understand the technical consequences of each choice? Undoubtedly, yes. But the patient has the final word that cannot be compromised by the physician´s personal opinions. Or else, we´re back to Tuskegee and Nuremberg.

And this is not just about end of life issues. Today´s medicine influences and interferes with human life before birth and goes beyond death, as *post mortem* IVF techniques prove, just to stay in one example.[35] And in the meantime, there are decisions to be taken, choices to be made, consequences to be beared.

Patient autonomy, then, is not just a moral imperative, but a fundamental right, designed to guarantee human dignity.

A defense of the idea that responsibility for one´s own acts has to walk side by side with rights, especially the right for choice. Therefore, we need to stop discussing so much about informed *consent*, and start focusing on informed *choice*.

In the precise words of Kristinsson,[36] "Personal deliberation might be valued for its ability to bring out, express, and create the distinct point of view of the individual in question, and for making it possible for the individual to steer the course of her life according to that distinct point of view. An individual´s "point of view" is a complex, dynamic outcome of emotions, judgments, beliefs, desires, habits, and character, and all of these are in turn affected by upbringing and other contingent circumstances".

We´re used to talk and read about patients' rights and medical liability, but it´s time to start thinking about shared responsibilities, to start thinking about patients' duties, since they´re granted the power of actually choosing how their life and treatment must be conducted. And with great power, comes great responsibility.

In the end, the unsolved issue is about healthcare decision-making. There are lots or arguments in favor of patient autonomy, and shared responsibilities, but they all raise new questions, from both an ethical and a legal point of view. Capacity and vulnerability are still the weak spots of the system, and solutions are to be found empirically, keeping in mind that medicine is not an exact science, and that there

---

35 For a better notion on the subject, it is recommended reading DANTAS, Eduardo; RAPOSO, Vera Lúcia. "Aspects juridiques de la procréation *post mortem* en perspective comparative Brésil-Portugal", *in Revue générale de droit medical,* n. 40, Bordeaux: Les Études Hospitalières, pp. 35-52, 2011.

36 KRISTINSSON, Sigurdur. Autonomy and informed consent: A mistaken Association?, *Medicine, Health Care and Philosophy.* DOI 10.1007/s11019-007-9048-4, Springer, 2007.

is still a long way to go regarding consent and choice, in order to provide respect to the patients and legal protection to the healthcare providers.

6. References

BEAUCHAMP, Tom L., CHILDRESS, J. *Principles of biomedical ethics*. New York: Oxford University Press, 1979.

BEAUCHAMP, Tom L., FADEN, Ruth R., *A history and theory of informed consent*. New York: Oxford University Press, 1986.

BÉNÉJAT, Murielle. "L´autonomie de la responsabilité médicale pour défaut d´information", *in Revue générale de droit medical,* n. 38, Bordeaux: Les Études Hospitalières, pp. 195-208, mar/2011.

BERG, Jessica W. [Et Al], Informed Consent, 2nd ed, Oxford University Press, New York, 2001

CALADO, Vinícius de Negreiros., COLARES, Virgínia. "Negligência informacional: uma análise jurídico-discursiva de precedente do STJ", *in Revista de Direito Médico e da Saúde,* Vol, 18, Olinda: Livro Rápido, 2010, pp. 7-37.

DANTAS, Eduardo. *Direito Médico*. Rio de Janeiro: Editora GZ, 2009.

__________ "Les différences entre le consentment informé et le choix éclairé comme causes d´exclusion de responsabilité civile dans la relation médecin-patient. L´autonomie du patient face au droit brésilien", *in Revue générale de droit medical,* n. 29, Bordeaux: Les Études Hospitalières, pp. 125-147, 2008.

DANTAS, Eduardo; RAPOSO, Vera Lúcia. "Aspects juridiques de la procréation *post mortem* en perspective comparative Brésil-Portugal", *in Revue générale de droit medical,* n. 40, Bordeaux: Les Études Hospitalières, pp. 35-52, 2011.

DONELLY, Mary. *Healthcare decision-making and the law.* Cambridge: Cambridge University Press, 2010.

FORTES, Paulo Antonio de Carvalho. "Um olhar bioético sobre as legislações brasileira e francesa relativas aos direitos dos pacientes à informação e ao consentimento", *in Revista Brasileira de Bioética*, Vol. 3, n. 01, Brasília, Sociedade Brasileira de Bioética, 2007.

KRISTINSSON, Sigurdur. Autonomy and informed consent: A mistaken Association?, *Medicine, Health Care and Philosophy*. DOI 10.1007/s11019-007-9048-4, Springer, 2007.

MANSON, Neil C.; O´Neill, Onora. *Rethinking informed consent in bioethics*. New York: Cambridge University Press, 2007.

McLEAN, Sheila A. M., *Autonomy, Consent and the Law, New York:* Routledge-Cavendish, 2010.

PEREIRA, André Gonçalo Dias. O consentimento informado na relação médico-paciente. Coimbra, Ed. Coimbra, 2004.

SALAKO, Solomon. "Informed consent under the European Convention on Biomedicine and the Unesco Declaration on Bioethics", *in Medicine and Law,* n. 30, vol. 01, Haifa: Probook, pp. 101-113, jan/2011.

SPRIGGS, Merle. *Autonomy and patient´s Decisions*. Oxford: Lexington Books, 2005.

SWITANKOWSKY, Irene S., *A new paradigm for informed consent*, Lanham: University Press of America, 1998.

VI

HOW INFORMED SHOULD CONSENT BE?
A BRIEF ANALYSIS ON CONSENT AND AUTONOMY UNDER THE EUROPEAN CONVENTION ON HUMAN RIGHTS AND BIOMEDICINE

Eduardo Dantas

Abstract: The so-called informed consent, as conventionally understood, is not synonymous with valid consent, because it´s just part of the process of enabling and respecting patient´s autonomy. Consenting is just a part of the process of choosing, and is not enough to allow patients to exercise their right to autonomy. This can only be accomplished through the complete and understandable disclosure of all information regarding treatment, their options and possible consequences. This paper aims to discuss how this problem is dealt with under the European Convention of Human Rights and Biomedicine, analyzing if the Convention really protects the nature of the procedure which is intended.

Keywords: Informed consent. Informed choice. Right to information. Informational negligence. Autonomy.

Summary: **1.** Introduction. **2.** Bioethics and the legal development of the principle of patient´s autonomy. **3.** Informed Consent, the duty to inform and informed choice. **4.** Autonomy and Consent to medical treatment under the European Convention on Human Rights and Biomedicine. **5.** Closing remarks. **6.** References.

1. Introduction

The last six decades changed our views on the relationship between a physician and his patients. The paternalistic component lost most of its importance (and in some cases, its almost divine aspect), and autonomy began to be seen as a key element for treatment and research using human subjects.

One of the most important modern documents that provided philosophical foundations for the moral justification of this shift in medical ethics was the *Belmont Report*, published in 1979 by the North American National Comission for the Protection of Human Subjects of Biomedical and Behavioral Research, as a response to the debates generated after some landmark cases, such as Nuremberg and Tuskegee, discussed below.

Among other issues, the Report stated that "to respect autonomy is to give weight to autonomous persons´ considered opinions and choices while refraining from obstructing their actions unless they are clearly detrimental to others. To show lack of respect for an autonomous agente is to repudiate that person´s considered judgments, to deny an individual the freedom to act on those considered judgments, or to withhold information necessary to make a considered judgment, when there are no compelling reasons to do so".

When one speaks about the right to information in the healthcare context, there is an almost automatic association to the expression "informed consent". It is virtually unanimous nowadays in modern society the idea that every medical intervention or experiment must be previously understood and consented by the patient or subject of research, in order to prevent liability.

It wasn´t always like this. To a better understanding of the present situation, it is important to look at it with a historic perspective. The first centuries of medicine were defined by a dichotomy of presumed superiority between the guardians of the medical knowledge, and the patients. The art of medicine was seen as something divine, almost supernatural, and little or no questioning was allowed regarding the decisions and commands issued by those few men of science.

The concept that the patient – as a human being – was entitled to certain rights, began to grow after the French Revolution, and later, after the Industrial Revolution. The physicians were slowly stripped of their divine origin, being regarded as a normal citizen, an ordinary professional, subject thus to failure and questioning.

Philosophers like Immanuel Kant *(Foundations of the Metaphysics of Morals) and* John Stuart Mill *(On Liberty)* developed the idea of respect for autonomy, recognizing, through the Kantian notion of *categorical imperatives* that autonomy was inherent to the human condition, thus forcing society to prevent treating patients as means to an end, since their individuality was an end in itself.

Mill[1] even stated that "the only purpose for which power can be rightfully exercised over any member of a civilised community, against his will, is to prevent harm to others. His own good, either physical or moral, is not a sufficient warrant... Over himself, over his own body and mind the individual is sovereign".

Not by chance, the second half of the eighteenth century saw the first statement coming from a legal decision, in the famous *Slater v Baker and Stapleton*[2] case, in which the doctors were found guilty of performing treatment, refracturing the patient´s legs, without his previous knowledge and consent.

At the same time, and for several reasons, in the subsequent years medical services began to lose the personal touch, surrendering to the market and the image of the doctor became something distant and unknown to the patient, raising legal issues about criminal, civil, and ethical responsibility, establishing the grounds for the informed consent doctrine in the patient-doctor relationship.

2. Bioethics and the legal development of the principle of patient´s autonomy

Since the end of World War II, the bioethical concept of patient autonomy[3] has gained importance,[4] shifting the centuries-

---

1 *On Liberty*, ed. Gertrude Himmelfarb (Harmondsworth: Penguin, 1974), p. 71. *Apud* SALAKO, Solomon. "Informed consent under the European Convention on Biomedicine and the Unesco Declaration on Bioethics", *in Medicine and Law,* n. 30, vol. 01, Haifa: Probook, pp. 101-113, jan/2011.

2 (1967) 2 Wils KB359, 95 ER 860.

3 "Autonomy is a form of personal liberty of action where the individual determines his or her own course of action in accordance with a plan chosen by himself or herself. The autonomous person is one who not only deliberates about and chooses such plans but who is capable of acting on the basis of such deliberations, just as a truly independent government has autonomous control of its territories and policies." Beauchamp, T. & Childress, J. *Principles of biomedical ethics.* New York: Oxford University Press, 1979, pp. 56-57.

4 "Respect for autonomy is the most frequently mentioned moral principle in the literature on informed consent, where it is conceived as a principle rooted in the liberal Western tradition of the importance of individual freedom of choice, both for political life and for personal development. ´Autonomy´ and ´respect for autonomy´ are terms loosely associated with several ideas, such as privacy,

old balance in the paternalistic relation between physicians and their patients.[5]

Of course, case law stating the importance of consent can be found in the anglo-saxonic jurisprudence since the late years of the 18th Century,[6] but it was only after the Nuremberg trials,[7-8] and moreover,

---

voluntariness, self-mastery, choosing freely, the freedom to choose, choosing one´s own moral position, and accepting responsibilities for one´s choices.". Beauchamp, T. & Faden, R. A *history and theory of informed consent*. New York: Oxford University Press, 1986, p. 7.

5 "Part of the explanation for the shift from beneficent paternalism toward autonomy lies in historical events of the twentieth century, primarily related to research, that called into question the trustworthiness of the medical profession. The atrocities revealed in the Nuremberg Trial of Nazi doctors, as well as highly publicized cases of human subjects abused in the United States, sparked suspicion of the general benevolence of physicians and researchers. In this context, informed consent was seen as a protection from abuse by untrustworthy professionals. Even if the medical and research establishment could not be trusted to conduct prospective review of the likely harms and benefits and to offer individuals only research and treatment opportunities that had acceptable risk-benefit ratios, individuals could safeguard their own interests if they were adequately informed and if their autonomous authorization was required before research or treatment could proceed. Individuals were thus called upon to exercise their autonomous decisional authority to safeguard their welfare". BERG, Jessica W. [Et Al], Informed Consent, 2nd ed, Oxford University Press, New York, 2001, p. 20.

6 Slater *v.* Baker and Stapleton, 2 Wils. K.B. 358 (1767). In this case, the plaintiff hired the defendants to remove the bandages from his fractured leg. Against the patient´s will and in spit of his protests, both physicians decided to refracture the plaintiff´s leg and place it in an experimental device to stretch and straighten it during rehealing. In the reasoning, the Court stated: "In answer to this, it appears from the evidence of the surgeons that it was improper to disunite the callous [bony material in healing] without consent; this is the usage and law of surgeons: then it was ignorance and unskillfulness in that very particular, to do contrary to the rule of the profession, what no surgeon ought to have done; and indeed it is reasonable that a patient should be told what is about to be done to him, that he may courage and put himself in such a situation as to enable him to undergo the operation".

7 For more detailed information, it is recommended reading Norbert Ehrenfreund´s "The Nuremberg Legacy: How the Nazi War Crimes Trials changed the course of history" (2007, Palgrave Macmillan); Robert E. Conot´s "Justice at Nuremberg" (1993, Basic Books); and Michael R. Marrus´ "The Nuremberg War Crimes Trial, 1945-46: A documentary history"(1997, Bedford/St. Martin´s).

8 The Nuremberg Code (http://www.cirp.org/library/ethics/nuremberg/) states in its article first that "The voluntary consent of the human subject is absolutely essential. This means that the person involved should have legal capacity to give consent; should be so situated as to be able to exercise free power of choice, without the intervention of any element of force, fraud, deceit, duress, over-

the Tuskegee´s experiments,[9] that informed consent became one of the pillars of modern medicine, and almost the Holy Grail of medical ethics.

The foundations of this doctrine can be found mostly in the North-American case law jurisprudence, though. In 1905, the leading case Mohr vs. Williams[10] raised the issue wheter the patient gives a physician specific consent to operate, does the physician have general consent to perform other surgical operations undertaken to treat other problems? In this case, the patient arranged for the physician, an ear specialist, to perform surgery on her right ear After Williams began performing the operation he decided that Mohr's left ear rather than her right ear required surgery, although the condition was not life threatening. Williams operated successfully on the left ear without having received permission from Mohr.

Mohr sued Williams for battery and the court decided that when a doctor obtains a patient's specific consent for a particular operation he may not perform another operation on the patient without her consent. A patient's consent is implied when an emergency situation

reaching, or other ulterior form of constraint or coercion; and should have sufficient knowledge and comprehension of the elements of the subject matter involved as to enable him to make an understanding and enlightened decision. This latter element requires that before the acceptance of an affirmative decision by the experimental subject there should be made known to him the nature, duration, and purpose of the experiment; the method and means by which it is to be conducted; all inconveniences and hazards reasonably to be expected; and the effects upon his health or person which may possibly come from his participation in the experiment. The duty and responsibility for ascertaining the quality of the consent rests upon each individual who initiates, directs, or engages in the experiment. It is a personal duty and responsibility which may not be delegated to another with impunity."

9 Again, for more information, it is recommended reading Susan M. Reverby´s "Examining Tuskegee: The infamous Syphilis Study and its legacy" (2009, The University of North Carolina Press), with an analysis of the notorious study of untreated syphilis, which took place in and around Tuskegee, Alabama, from the 1930s through the 1970s. The study involved hundreds of African American men, most of whom were told by the doctors from the U.S. Public Health Service that they were being treated, not just watched, for their late-stage syphilis; and from the same author, "Tuskegee´s truths: Rethinking the Tuskegee Syphilis study" (2000, The University of North Carolina Press).

10 1905, Mohr *v*. Williams, 104 N.W. 12

arises. However, this does not allow the doctor a free license to attempt to remedy all problems found that are not life threatening. The court held that in this case, there was no evidence that the condition of the plaintiff's left ear presented a serious or life threatening situation.

Even though there was no showing that he had a wrongful intent or that he had been negligent, Williams was still liable for battery.[11] The court held that it was not relevant that the operation was successful.

The same understanding was reinforced in 1914 in the United States, during the leading case of *Schoendorff v. Society of New York Hospitals,*[12] discussing a situation where the patient had undergone surgical intervention without his previous consent. The New York Court held accountable the hospital for violating the patient´s body integrity, in spite of the positive outcome. Justice Benjamin Cardozo stated in his ruling that "every human being of adult years and sound mind has a right to determine what shall be done with his own body", words that became paramount for the informed consent doctrine with the passing of the years.

The expression "informed consent" appeared for the first time in 1957, in the leading case Salgo *vs.* Leland Stanford Junior University Board of Trustees,[13] dealing with a malpractice case where the patient found himself paralyzed in his lower members after a surgical procedure, without being informed of such possibility as a risk. The case decided that proper consent required provision of information. In the ruling, the judges decided that the physician has the duty to **disclose "*any* facts** *which are necessary to form the basis of an intelligent consent by the patient to the proposed treatment*".

In the French doctrine, one of the first trials regarding patient´s rights happened in 1942, and not by chance deals with consent issues.[14]

---

11 "The free citizen's first and great right – the right to himself .... this right necessarily forbids a physician .... to violate without permission the bodily integrity of his patient"

12 Schoendorff v. Society of New York Hospital, 106 N.E. 93 (N.Y. 1914)

13 Salgo *v.* Leland Stanford Jr. University Board of Trustees, 317 P.2d. 170 (Cal. App. 1957)

14 Cf. André Pereira, *in* O consentimento informado na relação médico-paciente, Ed. Coimbra, Coimbra, 2004, p. 61: *Cour Cassation,* 28-1-1942 *(arrêt* Teyssier): "... attendu que, comme tout chirurgien, le chirurgien d'um service hospitalier

The concept of *consentement éclairé* is widely spread in France, present in several laws, like the Law from December 20th 1978 (regulating biomedical experiences), the Law 94.653 from July 29th 1994 (inserting article 16, section 3[15] in the French Civil Code), and the 1995´s French Medical Ethics Code, reinforcing the evidence and necessity of respecting the informed consent doctrine.

In 1973, The American Hospitals Association were the first to implement the Patient's Bill of Rights which specified the right of any patient to receive complete and comprehensive medical information that he can evaluate and understand. The patient was given the right to accept or to refuse the recommended treatment after being advised of the consequences of his decision: "The patient has the right to obtain from the physician **complete current information** concerning his diagnosis, treatment and prognosis in terms the patient can reasonably expected to **understand.** The patient has the right to receive from his physician information necessary to give **informed consent** prior to start of any procedure and/or treatment[16]. The patient has the right to **refuse** treatment to the extent permitted by law, and to be informed of the medical consequences of his action."

est tenu, sauf cas de force majeure, d'obtenir le consentement du malade avant de pratiquer une opération dont il apprécie, en pleine independence, sous la responsabilité, l'utilité, la nature et les risques; qu'en violant cette obligation, imposéé par le respect de la personne humaine, il commet une atteinte grave aux droits du malade, un manquement à sés devoir proprement médicaux et qui constitue une faute personelle se détachant de l'exercice de sés fonctions...".

15 Code Civil, art. 16, n. 3: "Il ne peu être porté atteinte à l'integrité du corps humain qu'en cas de necessite médicale pour la personne. Le consentement de l'interessé doit être recueilli préalablement dans le cas ou son état rend nécessaire une intervention thérapeutique à laquelle il n'est pas à même de consentir".

16 A physician should convey the risks of an operation when a reasonable person would be likely to attach significance to the risk in deciding whether or not to forgo the proposed therapy. The standard measuring performance of the duty to disclose is conduct which is reasonable under the circumstances. There are two exceptions to this general rule: (1) where the patient is unconscious and harm from a failure to treat is greater than any harm threatened by the proposed treatment; and (2) where disclosing the risk to the patient poses a threat to the patient´s well being.

Another North-American leading case followed in the same direction. *Canterbury vs. Spence,*[17] from 1972. Its historical relevance lies on the demonstration of the imperative necessity of the patient´s understanding of the information transmitted by the doctor before a surgical intervention. In this case, the patient, who developed a paralysis after a laminectomy hasn´t been informed of a 1% risk possibility of occurring such side effect. The Court ruled that:

> "A physician is under a duty to treat his patient skillfully but proficiency in diagnosis and therapy is not the full measure of his responsibility. The cases demonstrate that the physician is under an obligation to communicate specific information to the patient when the exigencies of reasonable care call for it. Due care may require a physician perceiving symptoms of bodily abnormality to alert the patient to the condition. It may call upon the physician confronting an ailment which does not respond to his ministrations to inform the patient thereof. It may command the physician to instruct the patient as to any limitations to be presently observed for his own welfare, and as to any precautionary therapy he should seek in the future. It may oblige the physician to advise the patient of the need for or desirability of any alternative treatment promising greater benefit than that being pursued. Just as plainly, due care normally demands that the physician warn the patient of any risks to his well-being which contemplated therapy may involve.
> (...)
> In our view, the patient's right of self-decision shapes the boundaries of the duty to reveal. That right can be effectively exercised only if the patient possesses enough information to enable an intelligent choice. The scope of the physician's communications to the patient, then, must be measured by the patient's need, and that need is the information material to the decision. Thus the test for determining whether a particular peril must be divulged is its materiality to the patient's decision: all risks potentially affecting the decision

17 Canterbury v Spence, 464 F.2d 772 (DC Cir 1972)

> must be unmasked. And to safeguard the patient's interest in achieving his own determination on treatment, the law must itself set the standard for adequate disclosure.
> (...)
> The topics importantly demanding a communication of information are the inherent and potential hazards of the proposed treatment, the alternatives to that treatment, if any, and the results likely if the patient remains untreated. The factors contributing significance to the dangerousness of a medical technique are, of course, the incidence of injury and the degree of the harm threatened. A very small chance of death or serious disablement may well be significant; a potential disability which dramatically outweighs the potential benefit of the therapy or the detriments of the existing malady may summons discussion with the patient."

In 1989, deciding a case in the UK courts[18], Lord Donaldson MR stated in his ruling that:

> "The ability of the ordinary adult to exercise a free choice in deciding whether to accept or refuse medical treatment and to choose between treatments is not to be dismissed as desirable but inessential. It is a crucial factor in relation to all medical treatment".

3. Informed Consent, the duty to inform and informed choice

There are several legal issues regarding consent, and litigation is increasing in relation to consent issues. Too many aspects need to be taken into consideration for consent to be considered valid, such as when consent was obtained and whether the risks have been explained; moreover, whether they were understood by the patient (sometimes, cultural issues or language barriers can be a complication); whether the patient is a minor (if so, mature or not to decide by him/herself); whether an adult patient has legal capacity to decide (and also, if

18 *In Re F (Mental Patient: Sterilisation) (1990) 2 AC 1.*

having legal capacity to decide, clinical capacity is absent); whether an oral consent constitutes enough evidence that information has been given and understood. But above all – and that´s precisely the object of this study – whether the patients have been given sufficient, adequate, complete information, so that they can actually decide, and not just consent to a physician´s suggestion.

Very often, tough, physicians and health care providers misunderstand the concept of the so-called *informed consent.*[19]

Informed consent is the authorization given by the patient to undergo treatment, based on the knowledge of the nature of a medical procedure, and be submitted to risks, side effects, possible complications, benefits and alternatives to the proposed treatment. In other words, it is the acceptance of the services to be delivered by a healthcare professional, after understanding what is being consented to.

It is necessary to understand that the process of consenting constitutes, at the same time, a patient´s right and a physician´s duty.[20] The patient must be informed in a clear and comprehensible

---

19 "It is always an open question whether an autonomous person with the capacity to give an informed consent actually has, in any specific instance, given an informed consent, in the sense of making an autonomous choice to authorize or refuse an intervention". Faden, R, Beauchamp, T L, *A History and theory of informed consent*, Oxford University Press, 1986, p. 237.

20 Regarding this, see for example articles 22, 24, 26, 31 and 34 of the Brazilian Medical Ethics Code, issued by the Federal Council of Medicine as Resolution 1931/2009: "Art. 22 – [É vedado ao médico] Deixar de obter o consentimento do paciente ou de seu representante legal após esclarecê-lo sobre o procedimento a ser realizado, salvo em caso de risco iminente de morte"; "Art. 24 – [É vedado ao médico] Deixar de garantir ao paciente o exercício do direito de decidir livremente sobre sua pessoa ou seu bem-estar, bem como exercer sua autoridade para limitá-lo"; "Art. 26 – [É vedado ao médico] Deixar de respeitar a vontade de qualquer pessoa, considerada capaz fisica e mentalmente, em greve de fome, ou alimentá-la compulsoriamente, devendo cientificá-la das prováveis complicações do jejum prolongado e, na hipótese de risco iminente de morte, tratá-la"; "Art. 31 – [É vedado ao médico] Desrespeitar o direito do paciente ou de seu representante legal de decidir livremente sobre a execução de práticas diagnósticas ou terapêuticas, salvo em caso de risco iminente de morte"; "Art. 34 – [É vedado ao médico] Deixar de informar ao paciente o diagnóstico ou prognóstico, os riscos e os objetivos do tratamento, salvo quando a comunicação direta possa lhe provocar dano, devendo, nesse caso, fazer a comunicação a seu representante legal".

way, according to his cognitive capabilities, about his diagnostic, risks, prognosis, and existing treatment alternatives, even those the doctor do not think fit for the specific case.

It is also important to point out that the mere act of reading and signing a paper, a consent form, is not enough to release the physician from his duties, from his obligation to inform accordingly (even if this written form is an important piece of evidence of due diligence).

The right to be informed has nothing, or very little, to do with the true exercise of patient´s autonomy. The act of consenting *to* some treatment, research, experiment or surgical procedure is just part of a bigger process, where the patient can exercise its autonomy. Someone can consent (in the sense of agreement or assent), based on the trust put over the doctor, based on indifference, fear, or even *because* it didn´t receive all necessary information to really *choose* among different possible options.

Informed consent is often mistaken by informed choice – this last one being essential to achieve the fulfillment of the right to be informed (and the physician´s duty to inform).

The patient needs not only receive, but also understand the information that has been handed over, and not just simply receive it without processing it properly. Information without comprehension is legally void, because it could be proven that the patient consented (or signed a consent form), but did not exercise his right to free and informed choice. His autonomy would be jeopardized.

4. Autonomy and Consent to Medical Treatment under the European Convention on Human Rights and Biomedicine

Recognizing the need to establish boundaries to the evolution of biomedicine, and to create standard concepts for the protection of human beings in the field of health and biomedical research, the member States of the Council of Europe issued a declaration, defining rights and responsibilities to safeguard fundamental rights and freedoms of the individual. Among those rights, were the protection of autonomy, and those patients not able to consent.

Article 5 of the Oviedo Convention (European Convention of Human Rights and Biomedicine, 1997), clearly provides that "*An intervention in the health field may only be carried out after the person concerned has given free and informed consent. This person shall beforehand be given appropriate information as to the purpose and nature of the intervention as well as on its consequence and risks. The person concerned may freely withdraw at any time.*"

Very similar to that, and just a few years later, UNESCO´s Universal Declaration on Biomedicine and Human Rights (2005) recognized the same principle of respect for autonomy, also in its article 5: "*The autonomy of persons to make decisions, while taking responsibility for those decisions and respecting the autonomy of others, is to be respected*".

And what can be considered appropriate information? That is a difficult question, since the answer may differ, given the specific situation. But mostly, the communication between the health care provider and his patient must include the existing treatment options (not only the main options) with their purposes and details, their benefits and risks (commonly occurring risks and those unlikely to occur), possible side-effects, success rates, the reasons why an specific option is being recommended, the prognosis, and the risks of not having treatment. In other words, the information disclosure has to be relevant and reasonable enough to make sure that the exercise of patient´s autonomy is effective and meaningful.

That being said, the act of obtaining consent without allowing proper choice doesn´t represent an automatic release from professional duties regarding information, if this was withheld, distorted, tampered with, or incomplete. The physician would still be held liable for informational negligence.[21]

---

21 Regarding informational negligence, France had a particular prolific year in 2010, with important decisions issued by the *Cour de Cassation* recognizing civil responsibility and negligence for the breach of duty to inform the patient properly. For an overview of the French jurisprudence, it is recommended reading the decisions from January 28th, June 3rd and October 14th.
In Brazil, the Superior Court of Justice (STJ) also decided in favor of the plaintiff, holding a blood bank liable for lack of proper communication of test results (REsp nº 1.071.969/PE). In 2007, another case, involving plastic surgery (AgRg in Ag 818.144/SP) had a similar result, with the court ruling that "the physician who do not inform his patient about the risks of surgery is negligent, being liable for all damages resulting from the intervention". In the opposite direction, a case judged in 2009 (REsp 1.051.674/RS) exempted the doctor from being considered responsible for an unexpected result, because he proved the fulfillment of the duty to inform. All three rulings avaiable at www.stj.jus.br.

We have been stressing the importance of consent – and consent forms – over the past years, forgetting that there are more important situations to be dealt with, arising from the relationship in question. Let´s take as an example, article 5 of the European Convention on Human Rights and Biomedicine (the Oviedo Convention), as previously stated here. All attention is drawn to the first part of the text, which says that "*an intervention in the health field may only be carried out after the person concerned has given free and informed consent to it*". However, the key to understand the true spirit of the law lies in the second part of the article, which states that "*this person shall beforehand be given appropriate information as to the purpose and nature of the intervention as well as on its consequences and risks*".

Again, UNESCO´s Universal Declaration on Biomedicine and Human Rights imposes the same need for information disclosure in its article 6, which states that "*Any preventive, diagnostic and therapeutic medical intervention is only to be carried out with the prior, free and informed consent of the person concerned, based on adequate information. The consent should where appropriate, be express and may be withdrawn by the person concerned at any time and for any reason without disadvantage or prejudice*".

In the same direction, Sheila McLean[22] highlights the importance of information in the process of consenting and choosing:

> "One way, it seems obvious, that we can facilitate the making of a valid choice, is by ensuring that the patient is provided with the wherewithal to make a decision in the first place. In other words, the patient needs information on which to base his or her choice. The "informed", or more accurately informational, aspect of consent is the element that focuses on the patient´s right to receive relevant and sufficient information in order to enable him or her to make a decision. It is generally assumed, then, that – in the absence of a competent refusal to receive any information that might be offered – a valid consent (or refusal) depends

22 McLean, Sheila A. M., *Autonomy, Consent and the Law*, Routledge-Cavendish, 2010, p. 42

> on the sharing of information with the patient. The doctor is, therefore, under an obligation to share information with his or her patient."

Appropriate information seems to be the main element about patient´s autonomy rights. The information, to be "appropriate", does NOT need to meet the doctor´s assessment of the situation, but the patient´s. All relevant data, alternatives (even those the physician thinks are not recommended to the case, based on its experience) and risks must be disclosed to the patient, in an understandable way, in order to provide sufficient elements for a decision – a choice – to be made. This – and not consenting – is the real exercise of autonomy. These exact same ideas are exposed in article 5[23] of the Inter American Convention of Human Rights (1969).

As a matter of comparative law, in the U.S., the *Patient Self-determination Act* (1991) regulates the idea of the right to information as a basic requirement, being the right to informed consent just a part of the process, not its final goal. A consent form signed by the patient is not a safeguard from lawsuits. Of course, it´s an important document, but cannot be seen as the only thing that matters in defensive medicine.

The examples of legal documents could go on and on, in Brazil,[24] Portugal,[25] Spain,[26] France[27] and Israel,[28] and all over the world, showing that there is a new way of dealing with old dilemmas, and that

23 Article 5. Right to Humane Treatment – 1.Every person has the right to have his physical, mental, and moral integrity respected.

24 In Brazil, Federal laws, such as Law 8.080/1990 (Consumer´s Defense Code) article 7, section V, reinforces to the patient the right to information about his/her health conditions; Law 10.741/2003 (Elderly´s Protection Act) ensures the right to choose the most favourable health treatment; Law 9.434/1997 (Organ and Tissues Transplantation) requires consent for every procedure. State Law salso regulates patient´s rights, such as Law 10.204/1999 (São Paulo); Law 14.254/2003 (Paraná); and Law 16.279/2006 (Minas Gerais).

25 Deontological Code from the Portuguese Order of Physicians (Regulamento 14/2009), specially articles 44 to 51.

26 Ley 41/2002

27 Law of March 4th, 2002. And also, for example, article 1111-2 of the Public Health Code.

28 The Patient´s Rights Law, 1996.

health care providers have to adapt their concepts to the new ideas. The world has evolved, and that requires adaptation.

A patient doesn´t need to consent to a proposed treatment. This may come as a shock to many doctors, as they are trained to "fight" diseases, and save lives, no matter what. What they´re not taught in med schools is the fact that their main obligations – apart from acting with the best of their techniques and skills – is that they must provide information to the patient. The patient will decide, based on its personal life, values, morals and beliefs, which is the best option. Only then autonomy can be respected and enforced. These ideas are well explained in the words of Irene Switankowsky:[29]

> "The ultimate purpose of informed consent is to ensure that the patient makes an autonomous, rational, reflective, well-understood decision about a medical procedure or treatment alternative that s(he) believes will be most beneficial. In short, the ultimate purpose of properly informed consent is to protect a patient´s autonomy under all medical circumstances".

It is a mistake to think that obtaining informed consent – as it happens today in most of the cases – is enough to exempt the physician from liability, excluding legal responsibilities in the event of occurring an undesired outcome during the treatment or procedure.

A treatment or procedure can be considered successful from a clinical point of view, but later seen as inappropriate when confronted with other possible outcomes that could be expected if a different therapeutic method had been informed to – and chosen by – the patient.

This lack of information doesn´t necessarily means negligence. It may represent the expression of the physicians beliefs, based in his own experience or in the medical literature, that the proposed solution was the most adequate to the situation faced at a given moment. The problem is that this behavior goes against ethical principles and legal

29 Switankowsky, Irene S., A *new paradigm for informed consent*, University Press of America, 1998, p. 2

commands that consider mandatory the disclosure of all information available. Withholding information about alternatives may be considered – in a lawsuit or in a disciplinary investigation – an undue interference in treatment, thus breaching confidence and contrary to the principles of good-faith and autonomy.

This notion is no different in several jurisdictions. In fact, it represents a tendency towards autonomy, as can be seen in the words of André Pereira[30], when stating that "recently, some authors have been proposing a more comprehensive concept. The expression *informed consent* has been criticized in the anglo-saxonic doctrine, since information is but an aspect of proper consent (´comprehensive or enlightened consent´). Thus, the use of the expression *informed choice* is being suggested. This concept could comprise, among other aspects, information about the consequences of refusal or withdrawing consent, therapeutic alternatives, choice of medicinal products (implicating changes in the regulatory frame of advertisement, choice of medical facilities, etc.). In the Portuguese law, it is well established the right to "information on the existing health services" and the "right to free choice of physician", and also the right to a "second opinion". All these aspects considered, they go beyond simple informed consent; they are advanced expressions of the right to an informed consent, in the modern version of *informed choice*: self-determination in health care implies not only patient´s consent or refusal to a proposed intervention, but in possessing all elements to analyze treatment possibilities in medical, chirurgical and pharmaceutical field".[31]

30 Pereira, André, *O consentimento informado na relação médico-paciente*, Ed. Coimbra, Coimbra, 2004, p. 74.

31 Translated from the original "Mais recentemente, alguns autores vêm propondo um conceito mais abrangente. Assim, na doutrina anglo-saxônica critica-se a expressão *informed consent*, visto que a informação é apenas um aspecto do consentimento esclarecido ("*comprehensive or enlightened consent*"). Assim, vem sendo proposta a utilização da expressão *informed choice*. Este conceito teria a virtude de abranger, entre outros aspectos, a informação sobre as conseqüências da recusa ou revogação do consentimento, as alternativas terapêuticas, a escolha dos medicamentos (o que implica alterações à regulamentação da publicidade dos medicamentos, a escolha do estabelecimento de saúde, etc.). No direito português encontramos consagrado o direito à "*informação sobre os serviços de saúde existentes*" e o "*direito à livre escolha do médico*", e ainda o direito à "*segunda

The right to consent, as an attribute of personal autonomy, is fundamental to ethical medicine. Its components are: information disclosure, voluntariness, and competency. Breach of informed consent may be actionable as battery or as malpractice.

In other words, obtaining a so-called valid and regular informed consent may be considered void, if it is not a result of an informed choice, leaving the doctor vulnerable to the legal risks and to the unpredictability of the medical activity.

5. Closing remarks

> "To violate a person´s autonomy is to treat that person merely as a means, that is, in accordance with others´ goals without regard to that person´s own goals. Such treatment is a fundamental moral violation because autonomous persons are ends in themselves capable of determining their destinies."
>
> Beauchamp and Childress, *Principles of Biomedical Ethics,* 1994, 4th ed., p. 125.

Health care providers tend to think that the sanctity of life is the most important guarantee, and the most important fundamental right in modern constitutions in the western world. It´s *not*. Legislators – and philosophers – all over the world begin to understand *Human Dignity* as a fundamental principle. And that dying with dignity – choosing not to undergo painful treatments to prolong life beyond cure; choosing to withdraw useless treatment, leave the hospital and die at home, surrounded by family and friends instead of doctors, nurses and bipping machines; and even refusing treatments that would oppose deeply

opinião". Tudo aspectos que vão para além do simples consentimento livre e esclarecido. São expressões avançadas do direito ao consentimento informado, na sua vertente mais moderna de *informed choice*: a autodeterminação nos cuidados de saúde implica, não só que o paciente consinta ou recuse uma (heteronomamente) determinada intervenção, mas que tenha todos elementos de análise sobre as possibilidades de tratamento possíveis, no domínio médico, cirúrgico e farmacêutico.".

against a patient´s religious beliefs – is part of living with dignity. This is the fundamental right that must be enforced.

The physician´s obligation, then, is to help the patient in choosing what is best for him/her, providing complete and adequate information. Is the doctor more prepared to understand the technical consequences of each choice? Undoubtedly, yes. But the patient has the final word that cannot be compromised by the physician´s personal opinions. Or else, we´re back to Tuskegee and Nuremberg.

And this is not just about end of life issues. Today´s medicine influences and interferes with human life before birth and goes beyond death, as *post mortem* IVF techniques prove, just to stay in one example[32]. And in the meantime, there are decisions to be taken, choices to be made, consequences to be beared.

Patient autonomy, then, is not just a moral imperative, but a fundamental right, designed to guarantee human dignity.

A defense of the idea that responsibility for one´s own acts has to walk side by side with rights, especially the right for choice. Therefore, we need to stop discussing so much about informed *consent*, and start focusing on informed *choice*.

In the precise words of Kristinsson[33], "Personal deliberation might be valued for its ability to bring out, express, and create the distinct point of view of the individual in question, and for making it possible for the individual to steer the course of her life according to that distinct point of view. An individual´s "point of view" is a complex, dynamic outcome of emotions, judgments, beliefs, desires, habits, and character, and all of these are in turn affected by upbringing and other contingent circumstances".

We´re used to talk and read about patients' rights and medical liability, but it´s time to start thinking about shared responsibilities, to start thinking about patients' duties, since they´re granted the power

---

32 For a better notion on the subject, it is recommended reading DANTAS, Eduardo; RAPOSO, Vera Lúcia. "Aspects juridiques de la procréation *post mortem* en perspective comparative Brésil-Portugal", *in Revue générale de droit medical,* n. 40, Bordeaux: Les Études Hospitalières, pp. 35-52, 2011.

33 KRISTINSSON, Sigurdur. Autonomy and informed consent: A mistaken Association?, *Medicine, Health Care and Philosophy.* DOI 10.1007/s11019-007-9048-4, Springer, 2007.

of actually choosing how their life and treatment must be conducted. And with great power, comes great responsibility.

6. References

BEAUCHAMP, Tom L., CHILDRESS, J. *Principles of biomedical ethics*. New York: Oxford University Press, 1979.

BEAUCHAMP, Tom L., FADEN, Ruth R., *A history and theory of informed consent*. New York: Oxford University Press, 1986.

BÉNÉJAT, Murielle. "L´autonomie de la responsabilité médicale pour défaut d´information", *in Revue générale de droit medical*, n. 38, Bordeaux: Les Études Hospitalières, pp. 195-208, mar/2011.

BERG, Jessica W. [Et Al], Informed Consent, 2nd ed, Oxford University Press, New York, 2001

CALADO, Vinícius de Negreiros., COLARES, Virgínia. "Negligência informacional: uma análise jurídico-discursiva de precedente do STJ", *in Revista de Direito Médico e da Saúde*, Vol, 18, Olinda: Livro Rápido, 2010, pp. 7-37.

DANTAS, Eduardo. *Direito Médico*. Rio de Janeiro: Editora GZ, 2009.

__________ "Les différences entre le consentment informé et le choix éclairé comme causes d´exclusion de responsabilité civile dans la relation médecin-patient. L´autonomie du patient face au droit brésilien", *in Revue générale de droit medical*, n. 29, Bordeaux: Les Études Hospitalières, pp. 125-147, 2008.

DANTAS, Eduardo; RAPOSO, Vera Lúcia. "Aspects juridiques de la procréation *post mortem* en perspective comparative Brésil-Portugal", *in Revue générale de droit medical*, n. 40, Bordeaux: Les Études Hospitalières, pp. 35-52, 2011.

FORTES, Paulo Antonio de Carvalho. "Um olhar bioético sobre as legislações brasileira e francesa relativas aos direitos dos pacientes à informação e ao consentimento", *in Revista Brasileira de Bioética*, Vol. 3, n. 01, Brasília, Sociedade Brasileira de Bioética, 2007.

KRISTINSSON, Sigurdur. Autonomy and informed consent: A mistaken Association?, *Medicine, Health Care and Philosophy*. DOI 10.1007/s11019-007-9048-4, Springer, 2007.

McLEAN, Sheila A. M., *Autonomy, Consent and the Law, New York:* Routledge-Cavendish, 2010.

PEREIRA, André Gonçalo Dias. O consentimento informado na relação médico-paciente. Coimbra, Ed. Coimbra, 2004.

SALAKO, Solomon. "Informed consent under the European Convention on Biomedicine and the Unesco Declaration on Bioethics", *in Medicine and Law,* n. 30, vol. 01, Haifa: Probook, pp. 101-113, jan/2011.

SPRIGGS, Merle. *Autonomy and patient´s Decisions*. Oxford: Lexington Books, 2005.

SWITANKOWSKY, Irene S., A *new paradigm for informed consent*, Lanham: University Press of America, 1998.

VII

Advance Directives: The Consecration of Autonomy and Dignity of the Human Being

Marianna Chaves

Abstract: Advance directives emerge in the doctor-patient relationship as a way to ensure that the autonomy of the patient is observed, prior to a potential state of incapacity. Thus, autonomy can be exercised ensuring patient´s dignity and self-determination. Advance directives yet have the power to drive the medical practitioner and his staff so that it is given the treatment and care previously chosen by the patient. The main purpose of this paper is to show the lack of legislation on the matter in Brazil versus the recognition of Advance Directives by the Brazilian Federal Council of Medicine. Can a mere resolution of the Council transform directives into enforceable wishes? This is an answer we intend to offer throughout the text.

Keywords: Advance directives; Autonomy; Human dignity; Brazil

Summary: **1.** Introduction. **2.** The Advance Directives in the Brazilian system. **3.** Founding principles of the Advance Directives; **3.1.** Human dignity; **3.2.** Autonomy. **4.** The conclusion of a right to a dignified death. **5.** References.

1. Introduction

We intend to analyze the right that every individual has to decide in advance about the end of his life, choosing what seems best and most convenient, before being affected by incurable disease, in end-stage, or irreversible incapacity and being unable to express his will regarding how he wants to spend his last moments of life and which treatments he wishes or do not wish to receive.

In Brazil, the doctrine had already been understanding that there is a possibility for a person to express himself – in a document that holds resemblance with the will –by way of a declaration of will, about procedures or decisions regarding their own body or their life and future decisions to be taken when suffering from serious illness or unconsciousness – the so called living will.

André Pereira conceptualized the living will as a document written by a person of legal age and capable, generally in the presence of witnesses, that contains directives regarding the treatment in the last moments of life, having in sight eventual situations of incapacity to make decisions for and about him.[1]

Much has been criticized the nomenclature used, considering that in the Brazilian legal system, the will is a typical institute *mortis causa*.[2] Considering that the document in question has efficacy in life, the terminology "Advance Directives" (AD) proves to be more suitable. The uproar over the terminological issue seems – apparently – to have come to an end after the emergence of Resolution n. 1.995/2012 of the Brazilian Federal Council of Medicine, which expressly provides for Advance Directives of willingness of the patients.

2. The Advance Directives in the Brazilian system

Recognizing the need for regulation and the lack of legislation on advance directives from the patient's will in the context of Brazilian medical ethics; Considering the need to regulate the conduct of the physician in front of advance directives; Pondering the relevance of the matter of patient´s autonomy in the context of the doctor-patient relationship, as well as its interface with the advance directives;

---

1 PEREIRA, André Gonçalo Dias. *O consentimento informado na relação médico--paciente:* um estudo de direito civil. Coimbra: Coimbra Editora: 2004, p. 240.

2 For a deeper critique of this terminology, see TARTUCE, Flávio. "A questão do testamento vital ou biológico – primeiras reflexões", In: *Novos Direitos Após Seis Anos de Vigência do Código Civil de 2002*/Inácio de Carvalho Neto (org.). Curitiba, Juruá, pp. 433-458, 2009, p. 433.

Emphasizing that in professional practice physicians may be faced with this ethical situation yet not covered by current national ethics provisions; Recalling that new technological resources enable the adoption of measures that disproportionate prolong the suffering of the terminally ill patient without benefits and that these measures may have been rejected in advance by the patient, the Federal Council of Medicine adopted, in 2012, the aforementioned resolution on advance directives.

The resolution is quite simple and its content is restricted to two articles. The key issue is to know if the content of the document may or not be enforceable under Brazilian law. We will try to provide this response later.

The first article of Federal Council of Medicine (CFM) Resolution (1955/2012) defines what are AD for the Council. The AD´s are defined as the set of wishes, previously and expressly, manifested by the patient about care and treatment he wants or does not want to receive at the time he is incapable to freely and autonomously express his will.

The second article of the resolution is a bit more complex than the first, since it deals with different issues relating to the same matter. The head of this article indicates that in decisions regarding care and treatment of patients who are unable to communicate or to freely express their will, the physician will *consider* their AD.

The resolution uses the term "*consider*" since a physician may fail to take into consideration the patient's or his representative´s advance directives that, in his understanding, are in variance with the precepts dictated by the Brazilian Code of Medical Ethics (article 2, § 1 and 2).

If AD's are in accordance with the Code of Medical Ethics, the patient's wishes shall take precedence over any other non-medical opinion, including family members (article 2, § 3).

The CFM Resolution establishes a mandatory way to formalize AD's. These desires are not required to be a notarized document such as a will, for example. They may be spoken orally to the physician that will register, in the patient's medical records, the wishes reported to him directly by the patient (article 2, § 4). This paragraph clearly emphasizes the importance of the doctor-patient relationship. But, obviously, in absence of a declaration before the physician it is necessary to have a written document.

In absence of AD's from the patient or his designated representative, family members, or if there is a lack of consensus among them , the physician will resort to the Bioethics Committee of the institution, if any. In its absence, and when he understands that this measure is necessary and convenient (article 2, § 5), he will resort to the Medical Ethics Committee of the hospital or the Regional/Federal Council of Medicine in order to base his decision about ethical conflicts..

Within the Code of Medical Ethics, two articles have particular relevance in this matter and harmonize with possibility of AD's. Article 24 states that it is prohibited for the physician to fail to ensure the patients' right to freely decide about their person or their well-being as well as exercise his authority to limit it.

Article 41 states that it is prohibited for the physician to abbreviate the patient´s life even if it is at his own request or his legal representative's. But the same disposition clarifies that in cases of incurable and terminal disease, the physician must provide all palliative care available without taking futile or obstinate diagnostic or therapeutic actions, always taking into consideration the wishes of the patient or, in its absence, his legal representative´s. In summary, we can state that there is an express prohibition to euthanasia, but an opening for orthothanasia in Brazilian legal system.

3. Founding principles of the Advance Directives

As previously stated, it can be said that there is space in the Brazilian legal system – within certain limits –for people to have their wishes of life and death, respected. In other words, to have their dignity honored in all stages of life, including the very end of it. But which are the principles that lead to the understanding that there is a right to a dignified death?

3.1. Human dignity

Human dignity is not a constitutional creation. It is, prior to any speculative attempt, a fact, just as the human person. The Brazilian Constitution, recognizing its existence and eminence, made it an exalted value of the legal order and one of the grounds of the Republic.[3]

3 With the same understanding, see SILVA, José Afonso da. *Comentário Contextual à Constituição*. 5. ed. São Paulo: Malheiros Editores, 2008, p. 39.

To clarify the meaning of human dignity as the foundation of the Republic, the Portuguese doctrine asserts that it is the recognition of the individual as the limit and foundation of political dominance of the Republic.

This statement results from historical reoccurrences of attempted extermination of human beings, such as: ethnic genocide, slavery, the Inquisition, Nazism, among others.[4]

It can be stated that the principle of human dignity is currently one of the supporting bases of modern legal systems. It is impractical to disconnect thinking about rights from the concept and idea of dignity.

Dignity is a term under which emerge a collection of other ethical principles and essential values such as freedom, autonomy, citizenship, equality and solidarity. . These inscriptions are the result and consequence of political struggles and achievements associated with the evolution of thinking, development of the sciences and new technologies. The notion of dignity and indignity is what made thinking, organizing and developing the human rights possible.[5]

Ingo Sarlet classifies the dignity of the human being as a distinctive and inherent quality of every human being. This makes him worthy of the same respect and consideration by the State and the community, implying, in this sense, a complex of fundamental rights and duties to ensure his protection against any degrading act and inhumane treatment. In addition to providing and promoting their active participation and co-responsibility in the destinations of their own existence, it must also ensure minimal existential conditions for a healthy life.[6]

Dieter Grimm asserts that the dignity as the condition of intrinsic value of the human being creates for individuals the right to decide autonomously about their existential projects, happiness, life and even

---

4 See CANOTILHO, J. J. Gomes. *Direito constitucional e teoria da constituição*. 7. ed. 5ª reimp. Coimbra: Almedina, 2003, p. 225.

5 PEREIRA, Rodrigo da Cunha. *Direito de Família*: uma abordagem psicanalítica. 2. ed. rev. atual. ampl. Belo Horizonte: Del Rey, 2003, p. 94.

6 SARLET, Ingo Wolfgang.*Dignidade da pessoa humana e direitos fundamentais na Constituição Federal de 1988*. Porto Alegre: Livraria do Advogado Editora, 2001, p. 60.

when this autonomy is absent or can not be updated, the person should still be regarded and respected for his human condition.[7]

Much we talk about dignity in the early stages of life but it is important to emphasize that the final moment of life is just as deserving of care as its beginning. Each individual should have the right to freely express their will about their end of life and it is the role of the legal system give effect to fulfillment of these provisions. In attention to the dignity, these wishes should take effect prior to the time of death of the holder of the legal interests life and willingness.[8]

3.2. Autonomy

To Luis Roberto Barroso, autonomy is the ethical element of human dignity. It is the foundation of the people´s free will, allowing them to get – on their own way – their ideals of good living and good life. Here, the central notion is self-determination: an autonomous person defines the rules that will govern his life.[9]

Merely to differentiate autonomy and freedom, the same author recalls that freedom has a broader scope, which may be limited by external lawful forces. But autonomy is the part of freedom that cannot be suppressed by interference from the state or society as it covers basic personal decisions. Therefore, autonomy is the ability of someone to make decisions and personal choices throughout life, based on their own conception of good, without undue external influences.[10]

---

7 GRIMM, Dieter *apud* SARLET, Ingo Wolfgang. "*As dimensões da dignidade da pessoa humana: construindo uma compreensão jurídico-constitucional necessária e possível*". *In*: SARLET, Ingo Wolfgang (Org.). *Dimensões de dignidade*: ensaios de filosofia do direito e direito constitucional. Porto Alegre: Livraria do Advogado, pp. 13-44, 2005, p. 34.

8 See CABRAL, Vivian Boechat. "O Testamento Vital e a Efetividade da Vontade do Titular do Bem Jurídico Vida", In: *Revista Brasileira de Direito das Famílias e Sucessões*. Vol. 28, Jun./Jul. Porto Alegre: Magister, pp. 22-47, 2012, p. 24.

9 BARROSO, Luís Roberto. A *dignidade da pessoa humana no direito constitucional contemporâneo:* a construção de um conceito jurídico à luz da jurisprudência mundial. Belo Horizonte: Fórum, 2013, p. 81.

10 *Idem*, p. 82.

The biotechnological and medical advances now allow a prolongation of life (and death delay) that can transform the process of end of life in an extremely long and painful journey. Undignified. That's where the autonomy of will has more relevance in this matter. Everyone should have the right to die with dignity and not be forced to suffer for a futilely prolonged period of time, deprived of the domain over his body.[11]

4. The conclusion of a right to a dignified death

As previously mentioned, in Brazil there is still no legislation regulating the matter. But are we thus in a total legal vacuum? A document containing advance directives would be legally null and void? It does not seem.

The suspension of futile therapeutic efforts have support in the Constitution (Art. 1, III and Art. 5, III), which recognizes the dignity of the human person as the foundation of the democratic state and specifically states that no one will be subjected to torture or to degrading treatment; In the Civil Code (art. 15), which allows the patient to refuse certain medical procedures; In the Organic Health Law (law n. 8.080/90, art. 7, III), which recognizes the right to autonomy of the patient; and in the Code of Medical Ethics, which prohibits the physician to perform therapeutic procedures against the patient's will, outside a framework of medical emergency of salvation, which is not the case of a patient with irreversible disease, which gives no response to any type of treatment.[12]

More than that, we can state that this "legislative vacuity" is at least temporarily supplied by the Federal Council of Medicine´s

11 In the same sense, see BARROSO, Luís Roberto. *A dignidade da pessoa humana no direito constitucional contemporâneo:* a construção de um conceito jurídico à luz da jurisprudência mundial. Belo Horizonte: Fórum, 2013, p. 109.

12 RIBEIRO, Diaulas Costa. Um novo testamento: testamentos vitais e diretivas antecipadas. In: PEREIRA, Rodrigo da Cunha (Coord.). *Família e dignidade humana*: Anais do V Congresso de Direito de Família. Belo Horizonte: IBDFAM, 2005, pp. 281-282

Resolution on Advance Directives that according to some doctrine[13] is hierarchically equal to the law as it complements the legal system, filling gap where the legislature was silent.

Finally, there is nothing in the Brazilian Civil Code that rejects the legal force of advance directives. According to art. 14 of the Civil Code, the validity of the legal transaction has three requirements: capable agent; lawful, possible, determined or determinable object; species prescribed or not prohibited by law.

So while the document that contains the advance directives comply with such formal requirements, it should be considered fully valid under penalty to affront several constitutional principles such as the dignity of the human being and freedom, embodied in the autonomy to determine what will be done with his body, within his notion of health.

In summary: the Brazilian legal system currently allows a person to dispose of his body and his life, within the limits of orthothanasia, which represents a significant advance in terms of autonomy and self-determination.

5. References

BARROSO, Luís Roberto. *A dignidade da pessoa humana no direito constitucional contemporâneo:* a construção de um conceito jurídico à luz da jurisprudência mundial. Belo Horizonte: Fórum, 2013.

CABRAL, Vivian Boechat. "O Testamento Vital e a Efetividade da Vontade do Titular do Bem Jurídico Vida", In: *Revista Brasileira de Direito das Famílias e Sucessões*. Vol. 28, Jun./Jul. Porto Alegre: Magister, pp. 22-47, 2012.

CANOTILHO, J. J. Gomes. *Direito constitucional e teoria da constituição*. 7. ed. 5ª reimp. Coimbra: Almedina, 2003.

DANTAS, Eduardo; COLTRI, Marcos. *Comentários ao Código de Ética Médica*. Rio de Janeiro: GZ, 2010.

13 DANTAS, Eduardo; COLTRI, Marcos. *Comentários ao Código de Ética Médica*. Rio de Janeiro: GZ, 2010, p. 99.

PEREIRA, André Gonçalo Dias. *O consentimento informado na relação médico-paciente:* um estudo de direito civil. Coimbra: Coimbra Editora: 2004.

PEREIRA, Rodrigo da Cunha. *Direito de Família*: uma abordagem psicanalítica. 2. ed. rev. atual. ampl. Belo Horizonte: Del Rey, 2003.

RIBEIRO, Diaulas Costa. Um novo testamento: testamentos vitais e diretivas antecipadas. In: PEREIRA, Rodrigo da Cunha (Coord.). *Família e dignidade humana*: Anais do V Congresso de Direito de Família. Belo Horizonte: IBDFAM, 2005.

SARLET, Ingo Wolfgang. *Dignidade da pessoa humana e direitos fundamentais na Constituição Federal de 1988*. Porto Alegre: Livraria do Advogado Editora, 2001.

______. "*As dimensões da dignidade da pessoa humana: construindo uma compreensão jurídico-constitucional necessária e possível*". *In*: SARLET, Ingo Wolfgang (Org.). *Dimensões de dignidade*: ensaios de filosofia do direito e direito constitucional. Porto Alegre: Livraria do Advogado, pp. 13-44, 2005.

SILVA, José Afonso da. *Comentário Contextual à Constituição*. 5. ed. São Paulo: Malheiros Editores, 2008.

TARTUCE, Flávio. "A questão do testamento vital ou biológico – primeiras reflexões", In: *Novos Direitos Após Seis Anos de Vigência do Código Civil de 2002*/Inácio de Carvalho Neto (org.). Curitiba, Juruá, pp. 433-458, 2009

VIII

Coming Home with a baby from Brazil: How to advise U.S. intended parents who go abroad to have children through ART

Marianna Chaves

Summary: **1.** Introduction. **2.** Medical exams, costs and health insurance in Brazil. **3.** The treatments and its costs. **4.** Gametes donation. **5.** Surrogacy. **6.** Beneficiaries of the techniques of assisted reproduction. **7.** Visa. **8.** Being born in Brazil and leaving the country. **9.** Conclusion.

1. Introduction

The idea of this paper is to offer a brief, but efficient overview of ART to intend parents who want to undergo assisted reproduction techniques in Brazil. There is no intention to exhaust the matter, but to offer a panorama, a sort of practical manual of the current status of ART in Brazil, that shows the exact sense of what the law provides, what are the advantages and dangers of using these techniques in Brazil.

Although many countries already have special legislation on ART, in Brazil there is no specific law on the subject. Currently, there is only a resolution (n. 2.121/2015) issued by CFM – Federal Council of Medicine that, however, is regarded by some doctrine hierarchically equivalent to a Law, since it complements the legal system, filling the gap where legislation was silent.[1]

---

1 See DANTAS, Eduardo; COLTRI, Marcos. Comentários ao Código de Ética Médica. Rio de Janeiro: Editora GZ, 2010, p. 99.

1. Medical exams, costs and health insurance in Brazil

First of all, it is interesting to point out what kind of procedures and tests the intended parents usually go through in Brazil, when they decide it´s time to make use of ART. Normally, before performing the first treatment, patients are usually seen in a long consultation, of approximately 3 hours. Before anything else, the different techniques of assisted reproduction and their indications are explained in detail. Then, already familiar with the techniques, the patients have their case evaluated. Usually they just pay for that first consultation. The remaining visits are already encompassed by the costs of treatment.

Regardless of the type of treatment, some tests should be performed.[2] Some laboratories accept health insurance. Others do not. Usually, physicians have their preferred laboratories (some are their own), but patients are not obliged to use them. In any case, concerning to foreign patients it is highly recommended that they seek whether their international health insurance covers the costs they will have in Brazil and if the places where they will do the tests accept this same plan to avoid surprise costs. The exams are:

Research for transmissible diseases, with blood group and Rh factor, is required by the National Agency for Sanitary Surveillance (ANVISA), for all those involved in the treatment (husband/partner, wife/partner, egg donors, semen donor and surrogate) through the following blood tests: HB-Ag, Anti-HBc (IgM), Anti-HCV, HIV 1 and 2 (ELISA), VDRL (syphilis), HTLV I and II, blood group and Rh factor.

Women who will produce eggs must do an *investigation of ovarian reserve*, so they can be stimulated with appropriate doses of hormones, shall do the following blood tests: hormone levels (FSH, LH, estradiol, progesterone and prolactin), held between the 1st and day 3 of the menstrual cycle (counted from the first day of menstruation). The test should be repeated approximately one week later, with the same laboratory, between the 8th and 10th day of the same cycle.

The woman, who will have the embryos transferred into her uterus, must undergo an endoscopic examination known as *hysteroscopy*, to

2 There are clinics that specifically bring these alerts on their websites.

make sure that conditions are adequate and in some cases even to make some small corrections.

Examination of the semen of the partner or donor with some days (at least 3 and a maximum of seven days) of sexual abstinence. For men that suffer from azoospermia (no sperm when he ejaculates), except those who did a vasectomy, is requested tests concerning the dosage of *FSH, LH, total testosterone, prolactin and estradiol in the blood*.

After the birth of the child, the insurance issue remains depending on the insurance company that the intended parents are clients, and on the physicians chosen. In Brazil, most of pediatricians and physicians needed for post-natal care accept international health insurances. But they are not obligated to. Therefore, as mentioned before, it is strongly recommended that the IPs check this before going on trip. That´s one of the motives why a legal consultant specialized in this area is so important.

It is also important to emphasize that a vast majority of Brazilian physicians have malpractice insurance. The overwhelming majority of policies – if not all – are completely silent as to the nationality of patients. Thus, we can state that such insurance covers malpractice related to foreign patients.

2. THE TREATMENTS AND ITS COSTS

It is necessary a very brief distinction of the most common Assisted Reproduction Techniques, and then bring up their costs in Brazil.

Artificial insemination – AI is a technique of AR in which the male genetic material is deposited directly into the uterine cavity of women. It may be homologous or heterologous. *IVF – in vitro fertilization* is popularly known as "test tube baby." The fertilization is performed in the laboratory and boils down to three steps: 1 – the collection of a woman's eggs, 2 – collection of sperm from a man; 3 – withdrawal of the required amount of sperm and performed the union of the female and male gametes, naturally or artificially, resulting in a pre-embryo or constituted egg. The pre-embryo will divide into two, four, eight, sixteen, and thirty-two cells and, when it reaches five to six days – already called an embryo – is placed inside the woman's uterus.

The GIFT – gamete intrafallopian transfer translates into the oocyte aspiration and transfer to the tubes, along with sperm. That method allows *in vivo* fertilization and is intended solely to women who have healthy fallopian tubes. *The ZIFT – zygote intrafallopian transfer*, is the technique that transfers of the zygote to the uterus 24 hours after the start of fertilization. That method does not have high success rates, because the embryo remains in the womb when it was supposed to still be in the fallopian tube. *ICSI – intracytoplasmic sperm injection*, occurs with the introduction of sperm directly into the cytoplasm of the egg through a needle.

When we're talking about assisted reproduction, one can immediately think about private hospitals, but as a curiosity, it is interesting to note that the Public Health System in Brazil must pay for such treatment. There are some hospitals that make treatment at a reduced price – for example, charging only the medicines – for people that have a proven scarcity. When it comes to a treatment free of charge, the waiting list can be up to 3 years, like at Hospital Pérola Byington in São Paulo.

The costs of the "classical" artificial insemination can fluctuate from US$ 800 up to 3.800, depending on the State and clinic. The IVF can vary from US$ 5.000 to 10.000 and finally, the costs of the ICSI treatment can fluctuate from US$ 8.000 up to 17.000, again, depending on the clinic and the State where the treatment is going to be performed.

3. Gametes donation

In Brazil, the donation of gametes – either egg or semen – cannot have a profitable or commercial character. In a way, it is an act that must be voluntary and has an altruistic feature. There is no law regulating donation of ovum or sperm, only the resolution CFM 2.121/2015 disciplines ethical standards for the use of assisted reproduction techniques. Thus, trading gametes is forbidden and the donation cannot be paid.

For example, a known sperm bank in Brazil[3] has the following information on its website:

3 See http://www.pro-seed.com.br

> "You can do much good to the lives of these couples. It may be their hope. Bring them closer to a dream; reinforce a bond for the couples. Your *solidarity* can give others the same happiness that your parents felt when you were born. *Donating* sperm is easy and painless. It does not cause any side effects and requires no effort. It is a *noble initiative* that can bring a huge happiness for you as well, an action that will make you the *anonymous hero* by helping to complete the life of a couple".

In summary and in a single sentence, are not and cannot be paid. In another hand, the couples do pay for this genetic material. The price may be encompassed by the treatment, if the material is provided by the clinic or the couple can buy directly from a bank, including from abroad.

As mentioned before, there is no law regulating sperm donation. But there are some rules put out by the banks. The man must have between 18 and 40 years and must pass through several prerequisites to be accepted by a sperm bank. He must respond to a detailed questionnaire, go through a series of exams (for AIDS, syphilis, hepatitis and other transmissible or inherited diseases) and gives at least five samples at intervals of five to seven days of sexual abstinence. Even after the material is stored, the clinic waits about six months to use it, to be assured that the donor is healthy. According to the rules of the biggest sperm bank in Brazil[4], the donor cannot be homosexual[5] nor have more than one sexual partner per year. All samples are analyzed for semen volume, sperm concentration, motility and morphology of spermatozoa and a report will be sent later after this examination. And, of course, he must agree with anonymity.

As the Resolution of the Federal Council of Medicine states, "mandatorily will be maintained secrecy about the identity of donors of gametes and embryos, as well of the receivers. In special situations, information about donors, for medical motivation can be provided

4 Albert Einstein Hospital´s sperm bank.

5 Out of curiosity, it is interesting to note that in Brazil, the homosexuals cannot be blood donors, situation that has been causing a lot of perplexity as far as Brazilian´s Constitution prohibits any kind of discrimination.

exclusively for physicians, protecting civil identity of the donor". Thus, a good friend or a relative cannot do that "big favor". Situations like we see in TV shows (i.e. *Brothers & Sisters*)[6] are not allowed in Brazil. At least, when it comes to sperm donation.

The Resolution also states that "the practices, centers or services that use the donation shall maintain, permanently, a registry of general clinical data, phenotypic characteristics and a sample of cellular material from donors".

Usually, the couple looks for a donor with the same characteristics of the intended parent. The choice belongs to the couple, but there are some guidelines stated by the resolution of CFM that the clinics should have in consideration. In its section about donation of gametes, the resolution states that "the choice of donors is responsibility of the unit. As possible should ensure that the donor has the greatest similarity and immunological phenotype and the maximum possible compatibility with the receiver". The semen from each donor can only be used to produce a pregnancy in every 1 million inhabitants. This helps explain the paucity of the most sought biotypes in Brazil.

In Brazil, it is even more difficult to get egg donors, as the aforementioned resolution CFM does not allow the marketing of eggs. Because of this, in Brazil, less than 10% of all treatments are performed with eggs´ donors. This gives an idea of lack of donors in Brazil.

So what some clinics do? Ovum donation, with some of the patients paying the costs.

Usually, the donors are healthy young women who also need to have treatment because they could not conceive naturally, because their husbands were infertile, in most cases. Besides the difficulty in getting donors, the cost is too high for the recipient because the donor makes two treatments, paid by the recipient, who gets the eggs produced in the first treatment. The second treatment, whose eggs are to the donor, is performed approximately 5 weeks after the first. The costs of the exams, the first medicine treatment, anesthesiologist, testicular biopsy and semen sample from the donor, if required, are paid by the donor. The donors and recipients cannot know each other, in this called shared donation.

6 A sister in law had as sperm donors two of her brothers in law.

Sisters, family and others who want to help the recipient can be donors if they perform a cross-donation, i.e. the eggs of a donor relative will be donated to another recipient that does not belong to her family that also have a family member to donate to the first recipient. For instance: A recipient patient "A" has a sister who is called "X" and another receiving patient "B" has a sister who is called "Y". In this case, the patient "A" may receive eggs from the donor "Y" and receiving "B" may receive eggs from the donor "X". Thus, anonymity is preserved.[7]

Being an egg donor can reduce your treatment up to the price of the drugs. For example, a cost of an ICSI can be reduced up to 60% if the woman is an ovum donor. As for the sperm donation, there are some requirements that the clinics demands to be an egg donator, as: Maximum age of 34 years on the date of collection of eggs; tests of Hormone levels of FSH, LH, estradiol, progesterone and prolactin, held in the same laboratory, between the 1st and 5th days of the menstrual cycle and repeated between 8 and 12th of the same cycle, suggestive of being able to produce good amount of eggs; be exempted of transmissible diseases; have physical, psychological and blood compatibility with the possible receptor; have Body Mass Index between 15 and 25.

It is also usual, as in the sperm donation that the donor respond to a questionnaire in which she describes her physical, personal, intellectual, and vocational characteristics; personal and family history of physical and mental health, past illnesses and other details of relevance. The donor may also deliver a picture of her childhood to be seen by the recipient, but without risk of being recognized by it.

In both cases, it is absolutely necessary that the donors have signed an informed consent form. *Anonymity is imperative*. Who donated eggs or sperm will have no parental rights over the child that comes to birth.

4. Surrogacy

We can understand surrogate motherhood as an agreement in which a woman compromises herself to generate an infant, and later

7 See www.doacaodeovulos.com.br

give him to another woman- in this case, a man- and abdicates all her rights over such infant, including the legal classification of "mother". [8]

As the donation of gametes, *surrogacy cannot have profitable or commercial purpose*. It must be done for free. In Brazilian territory, the Resolution CFM 2.121/2015 allows surrogate motherhood when there is a medical condition that prevents or contraindicates pregnancy of the genetic donor or in the case of same-sex unions. And, the surrogate mother must be linked to the genetic donor in a kinship up to the fourth degree, having other cases analyzed by the Regional Council of Medicine. That means that the surrogate must be the mom, the daughter, the grandmother, the granddaughter, sister, aunt or cousin of the genetic donor.

Regarding to foreigners: are they going to bring their relatives to be a surrogate mother? That is a great difficulty.

5. Beneficiaries of the techniques of assisted reproduction

The Resolution of the Federal Council of Medicine states that every capable person that had requested the procedure and whose indication shall not depart the limits of this resolution may be receiving AR techniques as long as the participants are in entire agreement and properly informed about the procedure, according to the law in force. It also highlights that ART can be used by same-sex couples.

Therefore, we can state that both single women and men, heterosexual and homosexual married couples and couples that live in stable union (or are merely dating) can be submitted to ART. Until recently, the problem did not reside in getting the treatment. It emerged (for the homosexual couples) when the child was born. Almost assuredly the child would be able to be registered by only one of the parents. The question was even more complicated when it comes to male homosexual couples.

Because of this scenario, the Federal Council of Justice enacted a Provision (n. 52/2016) that stated that the child of same-sex couples

---

8 It is basically the concept brought by RAPOSO, Vera Lúcia. *De mãe para mãe*: questões legais e éticas suscitadas pela maternidade de substituição. Coimbra: Coimbra Editora, 2005, p. 13.

born through ART could have the name of both mothers or fathers on he or she birth certificate.

6. Visa

As in Brazil prevails the principle of reciprocity, it is required a visa for the entry of U.S. citizens in Brazilian territory. For this purpose, the American citizens must get a tourist visa.

The required documents are: the original passport (valid for at least 6 (six) months prior to its expiration date). The passport must have at least 2 (two) blank visa pages; one recent individual passport photo; the visa application form, duly filled-out and signed; photocopy of round-trip airline ticket, print-out of itinerary or letter from travel agent/airline, confirming purchase of round-trip ticket, including dates of departure and return from Brazil; proof of means of subsistence, like bank statement, credit card extracts or other document proving the ownership of financial resources. This visa is valid for 90 days and can be extended by 90 days. The cost for each visa is US$ 100. The person intending to stay in Brazil for longer than 90 days must request at the Federal Police Department in Brazil an extension. The total stay in Brazil cannot exceed 180 days per year and the visa is valid for 5 years, with multiple entries.

7. Being born in Brazil and leaving the country

Article 12 of the Brazilian Constitution establishes that are Brazilian citizens those born in the Federative Republic of Brazil, even though child of foreign parents, provided they are not in the service of their country. Thus, a child born in Brazilian territory will be Brazilian, with the possibility of holding the double citizenship: Brazilian and American.

To register the birth of a child, the parents can head to the Civil Registry Post, which exists in many maternity hospitals in some States of Brazil. Or, they may go directly to the Civil Registry of Natural Persons in the hospital´s district. The documents required are: the yellow page of the certificate (declaration of born alive) that is provided by the Hospital; parents´ ID, in this case, the passport. If the parents are married, only the father or mother of the child can proceed, in possession of both passports and marriage certificate. If the parents are not married or are without the marriage certificate, both must attend with their passports.

It is possible, when parents are not married, attendance only from the mother, taking a paternity statement or the father, with the mother's consent to effect the registration. It is important to mention that, in this case, either the statement or the consent must be written in Portuguese.

Done that, it is time to apply for the child´s passport. The child will not be able to leave Brazil, unless it has a Brazilian passport and will not be able to enter USA unless it has a visa or an American passport.

To get the Brazilian passport for a child born in Brazil, the foreign parents only need to bring birth certificate and their identification (passport or a foreigner identification card issued by the Federal Police). It is also necessary that one of the parents hold a valid CPF (individual registration), to allow the issuance of payment slip of the Union (the fee of the passport) and make the electronic application of the document. The absence of one parent can be met by express permission of the other (with notarized signature by authenticity), judicial authorization or power of attorney, authorizing the issuance of a passport for the child. The passport fee is less than US100.

For the American passport, the father, mother or both must apply in the American Embassy or Consulate for a Consular Report of Birth Abroad. The CRBA is an official record confirming that a child born abroad of a – or both – American parents acquired U.S. citizenship at birth and serves as proof of U.S. citizenship. This service is provided at the Embassy or Consulate with jurisdiction over your state of temporary residence.

Both parents must go in person with the child and must submit the following documents: Application for Consular Report of Birth; Affidavit of Parentage, Physical Presence and Support (Only required when only one parent is a U.S. citizen); Passport Application; Brazilian original birth certificate; Marriage certificate of the parents (if applicable); Satisfactory evidence that the infant is a natural child of the mother whose name appears on the original birth certificate. This evidence can be materialized with medical reports, pre-natal care, medical certificates, etc.; Evidence of U.S. citizenship of their parents (passports); Brazilian passport of the child (if already issued); Passports of parents; Records of the hospital where the child was born. These documents would cost approximately US$ 300.

In summary: children of American parents – except those on diplomatic or official mission – born in Brazil, acquire Brazilian citizenship at birth and may also claim American citizenship. *These children have double citizenship and they are required to obtain a Brazilian passport to leave Brazil, as well as a U.S. passport to enter the United States.*

Finally, a full legal advice in this process could cost between 3 and 5 thousand dollars with a fixed contract or US$ 250/ per hour, with a minimum of 15 working hours, depending on the law firm you intend to hire. In any case it is highly recommended to have as consultant a law firm with experts in all these areas: family law, medical law, and immigration law.

These consultants could help from finding the right clinic to getting you and your baby leaving to the USA safely.

8. Conclusion

As relevant issues and main points, one can state:

Brazil has a growing and interesting "medical market", but still suffers from a lack of specific legislation; IPs can be attracted to effective treatments at a reduced cost compared to other countries, but there are many factors to be considered; just forget the idea of having bonds or even know your donor of gametes: anonymity is the rule.

To be a donor of gametes, the men must have between 18 and 50 years old, and the women between 18 and 35 years old, and in excellent good health, that can be proven through a series of medical exams required by the clinics, hospitals and biobanks; surrogacy will only be allowed if the surrogate is related to the biological donor; the access to the ART for homosexual individuals and couples is not a difficult issue to bypass and the establishment of filiation for Brazilian same-sex couples is no longer difficult as it was until recently.

If you intend to have a Brazilian child, prepare to drown in bureaucracy. Your son or daughter will be Brazilian and American. He/ she must have a Brazilian passport (to leave Brazil) and an American Passport (to enter USA). More than money, this part of the process takes time and patience.

Bottom of line: Brazil would only be a good choice for foreigners that want to be submitted to ART if they are completely aware of what the country can offer safely – in terms of possibilities.

IX

Gestational Surrogacy in Portugal and Brazil

Marianna Chaves

1. Introduction

Modern techniques of medicine have broken the seemingly inseparable link between procreation and sex. Human reproduction has become viable in the absence of any sexual act. Moreover, medical advances have allowed the fulfillment of a reproductive goal once thought reserved only for heterosexual couples; now this is possible for a single person or for a homosexual couple. In short, it is no longer essential that to have progeny, a woman has to be united – physically or emotionally – to a man, and vice versa.

Sterility or infertility is in fact a common health problem confronting modern medicine. Certainly this is a leading reason individuals and couples seek consultations with clinics and health centers to access assisted reproductive technology (ART). While this is an important motivation, it is not the only one. In addition to heterosexual couples affected by disease or disability that prevents them from reproducing, there are single men, single women, and same-sex couples who cannot achieve pregnancy without medical help. Thus, while we are living in times of many ethical, legal, and practical issues related to ART, there is an enormous diversity of opinion on all sides. Therefore, a fundamental (although adjacent) question must be asked: is there, effectively, a human right to reproduction?

We would answer this affirmatively. Reproductive or procreative rights are fundamental rights of fourth generation. In other words, there is a fundamental human right to have (positive right) and the right not to have (negative right) children. The procreative liberty is consistent with the right to freedom, equality, and nondiscrimination based on sexual orientation, gender, or marital status.

In Brazil, assisted reproductive techniques are open to any capable person. Portugal, however, had and still has very restrictive legislation, which leads me to conclude that the state does not recognize a right of reproduction for all people, even after the major shift with a law reform in 2016 (Law n. 17/2016 and Decree n. 37/XIII).

Although some countries are inclined to voluntary legislative abstention in this matter, this does not seem to be a viable solution for countries such as Brazil and Portugal, which are part of civil-law system. In both countries, the written law is highly important. Portugal already has specific legislation addressing the whole issue. In Brazil, assisted reproduction and surrogacy are possible based on a resolution of a professional agency – the Federal Council of Medicine.

The Brazilian solution is inadequate, as we will verify subsequently, because many legal gaps still exist. It is imperative to note that the impact of ART is not confined to ethical or medical issues. Human reproduction implies new dimensions and considerations of basic concepts such as moral and physical integrity of people, human dignity, monogamy, maternity, and paternity, among others. Besides that, it evokes new interpretations of traditional judicial rules (or imposes new rules). Thus it is not a matter that should be left to individuals and families, to medical deontology, to discussion committees, or to any other intermediate ordering. This is a matter of state responsibility. It is an issue of the highest public interest that requires legislative intervention.[1]

After these brief opening remarks, the purpose of this paper is to analyze the possibilities and legal restrictions imposed by Portuguese and Brazilian legal systems in the field of surrogacy in their territories.

---

1 Guilherme de Oliveira made equal considerations about the Portuguese system. The article is dated 1994, when legislation on assisted reproduction did not yet exist in Portugal. See OLIVEIRA, Guilherme. "Legislar sobre Procriação Medicamente Assistida", in: *Temas de Direito da Medicina*. 2. ed. Coimbra: Coimbra Editora, pp. 89-104, 2005.

2. Legislation on ART in Portugal

Law 32/2006, regulating the use of ART, was published in Portugal on July 26, 2006 and suffered a major reform in 2016. According to Article 2, the law applies to the following ART techniques: artificial insemination; *in vitro* fertilization (IVF); intracytoplasmic sperm injection (ISI); transfer of embryos, gametes, and zygotes; preimplantation genetic diagnosis (PGD); and equivalent or subsidiary laboratory techniques on manipulation of gametes or embryos. The 2016 reform introduced a new provision including surrogacy. Article 3 states that the ART treatment and surrogacy must respect human dignity and prohibits discrimination based on genetic heritage or the fact of birth as a result of the use of ART. Article 4 of the act advises that in Portugal ART is a subsidiary method, not an alternative means, of procreation (Article 4, n. 1). Thus ART can only occur through a diagnosis of infertility. There is also the possibility of ART for the treatment of serious illness or in the risk of transmission of genetic or infectious diseases or other conditions (Article 4, n. 2).

Assisted reproductive technology (including surrogacy) can only occur in public or private centers expressly authorized for that purpose by the Ministry of Health (Article 5, n.1). According to Portuguese law, reproductive cloning is prohibited (Article 7, n. 1). ART cannot be used to achieve improvement for certain nonmedical characteristics of the unborn child, including sex selection (Article 7, n. 2). There is an exception for cases where there is high risk of sex-linked genetic disease, which cannot yet be detected by prenatal diagnosis, PGD, or when there is a powerful need for group HLA (human leukocyte antigen) compatibility for severe diseases (Article 7, n. 3). ART cannot be used for the purpose of yielding hybrids or chimeras (Article 7, n. 4). The use of PGD techniques is forbidden in the setting of multifactorial diseases where the predictive value of genetic testing is very low (Article 7, n. 5).

Under Portuguese law, only married people who are not legally separated or de facto separated may apply ART techniques. A heterosexual couple that lives in a de facto union for at least two years also may apply for assisted procreation techniques (Article 6, n. 1). This provision only applies to heterosexual and lesbian couples. The techniques can only be used for the benefit of those who are at least

18 years of age and are not interdicted or disqualified owing to mental disorder (Article 6, n. 2).

Until 2016 no mention was made of homosexual couples (or single people). Indeed, when the Same-Sex Marriage Act was passed in 2010, there emerged great interest in how the legislation would apply to lesbian couples because the ART law mentioned married people rather than "man and woman" united in marriage. The Same-Sex Marriage Act of 2010 (Law 9/2010) was silent about ART, although it did ban same-sex adoption.

The National Council for Medically Assisted Procreation (NCMAP) rectified this problem, also in 2010. NCMAP is responsible for deciding on ethical, social, and legal issues of assisted reproduction in Portugal (Article 30 of Law 32/2006). In an opinion issued in June 2010, NCMAP stated that under Article 4 of Law 32/2006, regardless of the provisions of Law 9/2010, access to ART techniques was forbidden to same-sex couples, even if they were united in marriage. According to NCMAP, this ban should remain until such time that the national legislature mandates a change in a constitutional form.[2]

3. Surrogacy in Portugal

According to Law 32/2006, surrogacy is any situation in which a woman is willing to support a pregnancy on behalf of others and relinquishes the child after its delivery, renouncing all rights and duties of motherhood (Article 8, n. 1). Surrogate motherhood is only possible in an exceptional basis. In absence, injury or disease in uterus that impedes a woman´s pregnancy or when there is a clinical justification, surrogacy is authorized (Article 8, n. 2).

Gametes must belong to one or both members of the couple. The surrogate mother cannot be the egg donor (Article 8, n. 3). The child born through surrogacy is regarded child of the beneficiaries or intended parents (Article 8, n. 7).

Surrogacy contracts must be detailed and contain provisions regarding fetal diseases and malformations, and termination of pregnancy (Article 8, n. 10). Contract provisions cannot impose

2 Full report available online: http://www.cnpma.org.pt/Docs/CNPMA_Relatorio_2010.pdf Last access: 05/01/2017.

restrictions to surrogate mother behavior or impose rules that violate her rights of freedom and dignity (Article 8, n. 11). All contracts that violate these standards or those that are onerous will be regarded void (Article 8, n. 12).

Regarding gay couples or single men, some doctrine states the restrictions imposed by the State to the exercise the right to reproduction cannot (or at least should not) be based on any kind of moral valuation, linked to pre-judgments on the sexual, familial, or social behaviors of the person.[3] The Portuguese Act still affronts patently the principles of equality and non-discrimination. Indeed, the Portuguese Constitution states that all citizens have the same social dignity and are equal before the law (Article 13, n. 1) and further provides that no one shall be privileged, favored, prejudiced or deprived of any right due to ascendancy, sex, social status or sexual orientation, among other factors (Article 13, n. 2). Therefore, based on the Constitution of Portugal itself, I believe that this legal provision does not survive constitutional scrutiny.[4]

In addition to banning surrogacy to gay couples and single men, current Portuguese legislation also punishes civilly and criminally commercial surrogacy in particular. The law establishes that those who conclude profitable surrogacy contracts will be punished with a penalty up to two years imprisonment or monetary fine (Article 39, n. 1 and n. 2). Those who promote onerous surrogacy by any means, *inter alia*, through direct invitation or an intermediary, public announcement, are punished with imprisonment up to five years (Article 39, n. 5 and n. 6).

In addition to the criminal regime, those who resort to surrogacy (out of the legal provisions) – whether it is profitable or not – will be subject to an administrative fine. In the case of individuals, they shall be subject to a €10,000 to €50,000 fine. In the case of agencies or other legal entities, the amount of this fine can reach €500,000 (Article 44).

---

3 See RAPOSO, Vera Lúcia. *De mãe para mãe*: questões legais e éticas suscitadas pela maternidade de substituição. Coimbra: Coimbra Editora, 2005, p. 70.

4 As we stated before in CHAVES, Marianna. "Gestational Surrogacy in Portugal and Brazil", in: *Handbook of Gestational Surrogacy – International Clinical Practice and Policy Issues*/ E. Scott Sills (ed.). Cambridge: Cambridge University Press, pp. 225-231, 2016, p. 227.

Those found in violation of this law may receive the following accessory sanctions: judicial injunction; temporary prohibition of exercising activity or profession; deprivation of the right to subsidies, grants, or incentives granted by public entities or services; temporary closure of establishments; cessation of authorization; and publication of the sentence (Article 45).

4. ART Legislation in Brazil

Unlike Portugal, Brazil has no specific law concerning ART. Currently, there is only a resolution (n. 2.121/2015) issued by Brazil's Federal Council of Medicine (CFM).[5] Some doctrine regards this regulation as hierarchically equivalent to law because it complements the legal system and fills a gap where legislation is absent.[6] But the fact is that there is an urgent need to establish a specific law governing the matter in every aspect. The resolution only points out the ethical standards for the use of ART and is merely an ethical guideline to be followed by doctors practicing in Brazil.

It is important to note that even the physicians of Brazil want a legislative intervention on this matter. Health professionals of this sensitive area are not satisfied with only professional guidelines or their professional conscience. They agree that, ideally, a law must define what is lawful or unlawful with certainty. In times in which the liability of medical acts is increasing, they find some difficulty in cropping the boundaries of their art. So they understand that professional ethics is just not enough to legitimate scientific practice.[7]

In its preamble, the resolution highlights the importance of human infertility as a health problem, with medical and psychological implications, and the legitimacy of the desire to overcome it. It also indicates that the advance of scientific knowledge already allows solving

---

5 Full text available online at: http://www.portalmedico.org.br/resolucoes/CFM/2015/2121_2015.pdf

6 DANTAS, Eduardo. *Direito médico.* 3 ed. Rio de Janeiro: GZ, 2014, pp. 300-301.

7 Guilherme de Oliveira indicated something similar about Portugal. See OLIVEIRA, Guilherme. "Legislar sobre Procriação Medicamente Assistida", in: *Temas de Direito da Medicina*. 2. ed. Coimbra: Coimbra Editora, pp. 89-104, 2005, pp. 91-92.

several cases of problems of human reproduction. It also recalls that the Supreme Court of Brazil, in its 5/5/2011 trial session, recognized and qualified stable same-sex unions as a family entity (ADI 4277 and ADPF 132). Finally, it indicates the need to harmonize the use of these techniques with the principles of medical ethics.

Section I of the resolution establishes general principles for ART in Brazil and emphasizes that such therapies play an important role in solving the problems of human reproduction (Section I, n. 1). Moreover, the same section indicates that ART can be used whenever there is actual probability of success as long as it does not entail a serious health risk to the patient or the offspring. The maximum age of ART patients is established as 50 years.[8] There may be exceptions that will be analyzed from a technical and scientific perspective.

The resolution also establishes the principle of informed consent. According to Section I, n. 4, written informed consent is mandatory for all patients undergoing ART. The medical aspects of ART must be thoroughly explained, including the risks, the results expected, and the proposed technique. Section I, n. 5, determines that ART should not be offered with the express intention of sex selection (presence or absence of the Y chromosome) or any other biological feature of the future child, excepting cases of sex-linked disorders. Section I, n. 6, establishes that it is forbidden to fertilize human oocytes for any purpose other than human procreation.

The resolution also indicates that the maximum number of oocytes and embryos to be transferred to the receiver cannot exceed four. The decision on number of embryos to be transferred is made according to the following determinations: (1) women up to 35 years of age: up to two embryos); (2) women between 36 and 39 years of age: up to three embryos; and (3) women aged between 40 and 50 years: up to four embryos. In situations involving donor eggs and embryos, the number of embryos for transfer is determined by the age of the oocyte donor at the time of egg collection (Section I, n. 7). The resolution also dictates that in the case of multiple gestations after IVF, selection reduction is not allowed. (Section I, n. 8).

Section II of the resolution deals with patient access to ART. The resolution establishes that every eligible person who requests the

8 Age limitations did not exist in previous resolutions.

procedure (and who is not specifically excluded) may receive ART as long as participants are in full agreement and properly informed about the procedure, according to the law in force (Section II, n. 1). It is also indicated that the use of ART for same-sex couples and single people is allowed, respecting the right to the doctor's conscientious objection. (Section II, n. 2). It is also allowed the named "shared pregnancy" in female same-sex unions where there is no infertility (Section II, n. 3).

Section III of the resolution addresses standards for clinics, medical centers, and the services that apply to ART. According to this section, the practices, centers, or services that apply ART are responsible for infectious disease control and collection, handling, storage, distribution, transfer, and disposal of human biological material for ART patients. Credentials, as minimum requirements, are outlined as follows: (1) a technical director responsible for all medical and laboratory procedures performed, which will be, necessarily, a registered doctor in the Regional Medical Council of his jurisdiction; (2) a permanent record (obtained through information observed or reported by authoritative source) of pregnancies, births, and malformations of fetuses or newborns resulting from ART; (3) a permanent record of all diagnostic tests completed on cells/tissues transferred during ART; and (4) the records shall be available for inspection by the Regional Medical Council.

Section IV relates to donation of gametes and embryos. The donation will never have a profitable or commercial character (Section IV, n. 1), and donors should not know the identity of the recipient and vice versa (Section IV, n. 2). The age limit for gamete donation is 35 years for women and 50 years for men (Section IV, n. 3). Mandatorily, secrecy will be maintained with respect to the identity of donors of gametes and embryos, as well as for the recipients. In special situations, information about donors for urgent medical reasons can be provided exclusively to physicians, protecting the civil identity of the donor (Section IV, n. 4).

It is also established that practices, centers, or services that offer gamete or embryo donation shall maintain, permanently, a registry of general clinical data and phenotypic characteristics and a sample of cellular material from donors (Section IV, n. 5). In the region where the unit is located, the registry of births will seek to ensure that no individual donor shall produce more than one pregnancy resulting in a child of the opposite sex in an area of 1 million inhabitants (Section

IV, n. 6). The choice of donors is the responsibility of the assistant physician. It must ensure, as possible, that the donor has the greatest immunologic and phenotypic similarity and maximum possible compatibility with the recipient (Section IV, n. 7). Doctors in charge of clinical units and services (or members of their multidisciplinary team) are not themselves permitted to participate as donors in ART programs (Section IV, n. 8).

The resolution indicates that voluntary donation of gametes is allowed under the procedure known as "shared donation." In this situation, donor and recipient, both suffering from reproductive problems, share both the biological material and financial costs associated with ART. The donor takes precedence over the biological material that will be produced (Section IV, n. 9).

Section V addresses cryopreservation of gametes or embryos. It is established that clinics, centers, or fertility units can cryopreserve sperm, oocytes, and embryos as well as gonadal tissues (Section V, n.1). It is also indicated that the total number of embryos produced in the laboratory will be communicated to patients so that they decide how many embryos will be transferred in fresh, and the excess, if viable, will be cryopreserved (Section V, n. 2). At the time of cryopreservation, patients should express their willingness in writing concerning the status for any cryopreserved embryos in case of divorce, serious illness, or death of one or both partners and when they wish to donate them (Section V, n. 3). Embryos cryopreserved for more than five years may be discarded if requested by the patients and not used for stem cell research, as provided in the Biosafety Law (Section V, n. 4).

Section VI concerns PGD of embryos. It is established that ART may include the selection of embryos subjected to diagnosis of pathologic genetic alterations resulting in disease (Section VI, n. 1). ART also can be used for HLA typing of the embryo, with the selection aim of HLA-compatible embryos with a son or daughter of the couple who is already affected by disease. Stem cell or organ transplantation must be an effective treatment modality for such disorders (Section VI, n. 2). The maximum period of development of *in vitro* embryos will be of 14 days (Section VI, n. 3).

This resolution of the CFM also indicates that assisted reproduction *postmortem* is possible. However, there must be prior and specific authorization of the deceased for the use of cryopreserved biological material in accordance with current legislation (Section VIII).

5. Gestational Surrogacy in Brazil

Unlike Portugal, surrogacy is not legally proscribed in Brazil. However, the absence of specific enabling legislation makes surrogacy legally uncertain at present. While resolution 2.121/2015 provides for the possibility of gestational surrogacy in Brazilian territory, it is imperative to point out that this is subject to a number of requirements.

Section VII of CFM´s resolution establishes that practices, centers, or services of human reproduction can use ART to offer surrogacy if there is a precondition of a medical condition that prevents or contraindicates pregnancy of the genetic donor or if a same-sex relationship exists.

It is established that surrogate mothers must belong to the family of one of the partners in a consanguineous kinship up to the fourth degree (mother, sister, grandmother, aunt, or cousin) and in all cases must respect the upper age limit of 50 years. Exceptions, such as having a friend as surrogate mother, can be analyzed by the Regional Council of Medicine. (Section VII, n. 1). As with the donation of gametes in Brazil, surrogacy cannot have a profitable or commercial purpose (Section VII, n. 2).

According to Section VII, n. 3, in reproductive clinics the following documents and observations should be included in the patient's record: (1) informed consent form signed by the patients (genetic parents) and the surrogate mother (the resolution notes that in the shared pregnancy among lesbian couples, there is no infertility); (2) medical report with the psychological profile, attesting to the clinical and emotional suitability of surrogate mother; (3) a detailed (in writing) description by the attending physician of the medical aspects involving all the circumstances of application of surrogacy, with biological, legal, ethical, and economic data, as well as the results in that treatment unit with the technique proposed; (4) contract between the patients (genetic parents) and the surrogate mother (who received the embryo in her uterus and delivers the baby), establishing clearly the issue of child filiation; (5) biological and psychosocial aspects involved in pregnancy and childbirth; (6) the risks inherent to motherhood; (7) the impossibility of termination of pregnancy after starting the gestational process, except in cases provided by law or judicially authorized; (8) the guarantee of treatment and medical care, including by multidisciplinary teams, if necessary, to the surrogate mother until the postpartum period; and (i) the guarantee of the civil registration of the child(ren) by patients (genetic parents). This documentation must be provided during pregnancy. If the surrogate mother is married or lives in a stable union, she must submit in writing the approval of her spouse or partner.

6. Potential Issues Arising from Insufficient Regulation

As mentioned, the use of surrogacy here can only occur altruistically. In addition, it requires an established kinship between the commissioning parent and the surrogate. These features decrease considerably the scope of surrogacy permitted under the resolutions of the CFM.

However, it should be added that because of the lack of civil or criminal legislation prohibiting it, in actual practice, many women make their uterus available for "lease" through "contracts" or "agreements" without any legal validity. This fact creates risks and insecurities for all parties involved, especially to the unborn child.

The current Civil Code lacks any special laws or rules governing surrogacy in accordance with the CFM resolutions. There is no requirement that a judge or court must consider a contract under CFM´s resolutions. However, in the event of commercial surrogacy, certainly the contract would be considered void.

Conceiving a child and having a full-term pregnancy are special experiences. A pregnant woman is subjected to more and more prenatal tests, many of them invasive. A woman needs to have healthy habits and diet. The incontestable and violent hormonal changes in a pregnant woman's body can cause the most varied sensations and symptoms. Getting pregnant is a great adventure and can represent a major physical and psychological challenge. Why not compensate this act that is nonetheless altruistic? The surrogate may use her body to help others who have been unable to achieve the dream of parenthood. When the gestational mother delivers the child, any discomfort is certainly relativized because the result – having a child – outweighs any unpleasantness or difficulty.

An analysis of the ethics of commercial surrogacy is not the purpose of this paper. However, it is imperative to point out that even though the law does not prohibit this practice in Brazil, the resolutions of the CFM have been widely accepted as a guiding framework by courts. Therefore, a lucrative surrogacy contract would not have legal validity, and this type of contract would be unenforceable under Brazilian law. In case of disagreement of the parties, there would be no way to resort to the judiciary to require fulfillment of the contract (before or after the birth of the child).

For instance, if there is a clause establishing certain health and dietary behaviors during pregnancy, there is no way to force the surrogate mother to fulfill it. If the intended parents do not offset the medical expenses of the surrogate, there is no legal remedy for this. Finally, if the surrogate mother decides not to surrender the baby, for all purposes, she will be the legal mother because under Brazilian law, the mother is she who was pregnant and gave birth.

There are no criminal or civil statutes that punish the creation or the breach of commercial surrogacy contracts. Any dispute could have unpredictable results, especially if the surrogate also supplied the oocyte used to achieve the pregnancy (a practice forbidden by the CFM resolutions). Conversely, if the intended parents do not want to accept the baby after the surrogate's delivery, there is no judicial mechanism available to enforce the contract or to punish them criminally.

However, in case there is genetic linkage to any or both of intended parents, the court may decide that filiation should be established in their favor based on their intentions to become parents and consanguinity. Therefore, in commercial surrogacy, the parties will face absolute legal uncertainty. Even under the terms of the CFM resolutions (nonprofit character, donated eggs, and kinship connection with one of the patients), eventual litigation over the child´s parenthood could evoke problems concerning establishment of filiation and delivery of the child. In this case, it is more likely that a judge would consider the terms established in the contract (although, again, the contract is not enforceable).[9]

From the viewpoint of criminal law, there is no legal punishment for the person who does not comply with the surrogacy agreement.

---

9 As we stated in CHAVES, Marianna. "Gestational Surrogacy in Portugal and Brazil", in: *Handbook of Gestational Surrogacy – International Clinical Practice and Policy Issues*/ E. Scott Sills (ed.). Cambridge: Cambridge University Press, pp. 225-231, 2016, p. 230.

However, Article 242 of the Brazilian Penal Code criminalizes situations of (1) declaring the parturition of another person as your own, (2) registering as yours the child of a third person, and (3) hiding or replacing a newborn by suppressing or changing any inherent right to civil status. As we can see, there is a need to harmonize the Brazilian Criminal Code with the resolutions of the CFM. Anyway, one can assert that a surrogacy contract under the CFM resolutions would not be criminalized. The Criminal Code itself establishes the possibility of a judge not applying the penalty in the event of recognized nobility. But in a country whose order is based on written laws, there must be harmony and full compatibility in the legal system.

7. Conclusion

In Portugal, the matter of assisted reproduction (including surrogacy) is regulated in detail. Besides the deontological provisions, civil and criminal statues exist. Consistent or not with the current state of society and the advancements of medical assisted reproduction (and irrespective of compliance with the Portuguese Constitution) access to ART techniques is still restrictive. Surrogacy in commercial form is expressly prohibited in addition to being punished in civil and criminal contexts. ART and surrogacy are not allowed to gay couples or single men.

Based on the premise that reproduction is a fundamental right, we understand that none of the justifications for restricting the right to parenthood is sufficiently powerful to exclude a large number of citizens from exercising that right. It is hoped that the constitutionality of rules incompatible with precepts of nondiscrimination will be challenged in the Portuguese Constitutional Court or in the European Court of Human Rights. Until then, it is not prudent to look for surrogacy in Portugal given the legal strictness with which the subject is regarded.

In Brazil, the current panorama of surrogacy serves to demonstrate that deontological norms are important but cannot be the only legal support of a relation so special and nuanced. Obviously, these issues should serve even to inspire future specific legislation in Brazil. But it is absolutely necessary to establish civil and criminal law to ensure contract compliance in exact terms. Such a reality will give legal certainty to all parties and determine the penalties for any breaches, removing the legal decisions from arbitrariness and possible injustices.

The prevailing view, including among medical professionals, is that a legislative intervention is urgent in Brazil. In fact, even the CFM states this necessity in the explanatory memorandum of Resolution 2.121/2015. Regrettably, there are relevant bills that have been in the National Congress for years, although none of them has managed to be placed before a plenary session for a full congressional vote. Such a circumstance translates into legal uncertainty for all parties involved in the surrogacy process.

Considering Portugal and Brazil, I can say that in the former jurisdiction, there is quite restrictive legislation (and some may even be unconstitutional), but legal certainty is provided. In the latter case, there is greater openness and almost full access to ART and surrogacy, offered in the absence of any controlling legislation. What is better, security and unfairness or insecurity alongside uncertainty? In my view, neither is ideal or appropriate. Thus it is essential that Portugal enacts legislation in conformity with its Constitution and that Brazil provides legal certainty through civil and criminal legislation.

8. References

CHAVES, Marianna. "Gestational Surrogacy in Portugal and Brazil", in: *Handbook of Gestational Surrogacy – International Clinical Practice and Policy Issues*/ E. Scott Sills (ed.). Cambridge: Cambridge University Press, pp. 225-231, 2016.

DANTAS, Eduardo. *Direito médico.* 3 ed. Rio de Janeiro: GZ, 2014.

OLIVEIRA, Guilherme. "Legislar sobre Procriação Medicamente Assistida", in: *Temas de Direito da Medicina*. 2. ed. Coimbra: Coimbra Editora, pp. 89-104, 2005.

RAPOSO, Vera Lúcia. *De mãe para mãe*: questões legais e éticas suscitadas pela maternidade de substituição. Coimbra: Coimbra Editora, 2005.

X

Brief notes on the surplus embryos

Marianna Chaves

Abstract: Assisted Reproduction Techniques produce babies, and also produces all kinds of controversies. In addition to confusing issues relating to identity and meaning of parentage, and beyond the implications of the failure to regulate them, the new assisted reproduction techniques tap into a profound and deeply held set of moral values. In a not distant past it, wasn´t possible to create human embryos outside a woman´s body. Thus, the issue of what kind of protection should be granted to the first stages of human life were inextricably linked to the matter of abortion. With IVF, new and complex problems have emerged, raising the question on how embryos should be treated. The present *paper* aims to bring up questions about one of the most delicate effects of IVF: the destination of surplus embryos. From the start, one can say that an analysis of the dilemma of excess embryos reveals a series of theoretical and practical difficulties.

Keywords: ART – surplus embryos – power of disposition – destination – adoption – freezing of gametes.

1. Introduction

Around the world there are currently millions of frozen embryos.[1] While some are cryopreserved because couples are still involved in

---

1 RAPOSO, Vera Lúcia. "O dilema do rei Salomão: conflitos de vontade quando ao destino dos embriões excedentários", em *Lex Medicinae* – Revista Portuguesa de Direito da Saúde, ano 5, n. 9. Coimbra: Centro de Direito Biomédico/ Coimbra Editora, pp. 55-79, 2008, p. 58.

fertility treatment, many will never be implanted in these couples and are named as surplus, excess, spare or excedentary embryos. There is a worldwide debate about what should happen to these embryos. Brazil had in 2009, according to data from ANVISA, slightly more than 8,000 frozen embryos.[2] The numbers in Portugal revolve around 11 000 embryos.[3] In the U.S., today that figure is around half a million of viable embryos cryopreserved.[4]

Immediately a question arises: the eventual destination of these embryos, in addition to their use in scientific research or destruction itself would be a donation or a kind of *sui generis* adoption? The terminology on the resolution 2.121/2015 of the Brazilian Federal Council of Medicine raises this issue in contrast to the doctrine.

The question of adoption *versus* donation is nothing more than the outcome of the definition of being speaking of a *res*, of a human being, a potential human life or an innominate intermediate situation.

And more: it is true that ART should evolve in a way to ensure successful deployments without the need for fertilization of multiple eggs, or even to evolve the freezing and preservation of gametes. But in the meantime, which one is the destination of surplus embryos? Utilization by another couple? Disposal? Cryopreservation? For how long?[5]

In addition to the determination of legal status of the embryo, another question, almost concurrently emerges: who has the legitimacy of decisions about the destination of these embryos? These are some of

---

2 See PINTO, Angela Joenck. "Embriões congelados ficam sem destino;Brasil tem 8 mil". Available in: http://noticias.terra.com.br/ciencia/noticias/0,,OI4890076--EI238,00 Embrioes+congelados+ficam+sem+destino+Brasil+tem+mil.html Access on: 05/12/2011.

3 Data also from 2009 provided by Vera Lúcia Raposo, Assistant Professor to the University of Coimbra and researcher at the Center for Biomedical Law at the same University.

4 Data from: http://www.embryoadoption.org/ Accessed on 10/12/2011.

5 Problems also raised by GUIMARÃES, Ana Paula. Alguns problemas jurídico--criminais da procriação medicamente assistida. Coimbra: Coimbra Editora, 1999, p. 109.

the questions this paper intends to bring to light as well as present some suggestions and perhaps enthuse a debate as heated as the very matter in question. Finally it is to be said that the analysis will be restricted to the Brazilian law, with touches of American jurisprudence.

2. The recipients of ART

In relation to the beneficiaries of ART, the Resolution of the Federal Council of Medicine is limited to providing that users of ART could be, all capable people, who have requested the procedure and whose indication does not deviate from the limits of this resolution can be recipients of the techniques of assisted reproduction provided that the participants are in full agreement and fully informed about the same, in accordance with current legislation. ART is also open to same-sex couples. [6] Thus, in Brazil, single people, as well as heterosexual and homosexual couples have full access to assisted reproduction techniques.

3. The reason for the existence of surplus embryos

The collection of eggs is a procedure in which is required a surgical intervention with use of anesthesia is which translates into a risk to the woman in question and, obviously, cannot be performed frequently. This is a situation where, furthermore, there is some physical and sometimes psychic distress. For this reason there are the so-called *surplus embryos*, which are due to the desire to take the maximum advantage of the hyper-induction of ovulation.[7]

---

6 The revoked resolution n. 1.358/92 merely provided that users of the techniques of ART could be "every woman, capable under the law, who has requested and whose treatment does not deviate from the limits of this resolution. They may be receiving the AR techniques, since they have agreed freely and consciously in an informed consent document". Note that with the new resolution, there was an opening up of access of Assisted Reproduction Techniques to homosexuals.

7 See KRELL, Olga Jubert Gouveia. *Reprodução Humana Assistida e Filiação Civil*: Princípios Éticos e Jurídicos, cit., p. 127.

For a long time there was not a safe preservation and freezing of eggs at low temperature, which should be collected and fertilized right away, due to the impossibility of their conservation. Moreover, due to possible lack of success in the development of multiple embryos implanted, it was necessary to simultaneously prepare several embryos, which would be used each time the implementation and development attempts were fruitless.[8]

This was the medical-scientific panorama until a couple of years ago and very recently the "genesis of embryos, biological orphans of current science." [9]

4. Donation or adoption? Property or human being?

The Resolution n. 2.121/2015 of the Brazilian Federal Council of Medicine specifically deals with the donation of embryos. Donation. But is the terminology that is more accurate? The resolution of CFM has the title of its paragraph IV the donation of gametes and embryos. Is it reasonable to mix the donation of genetic material – pure and simple – with the "donation" of human life, or at least potential human life?[10]

---

8 See MACHADO MACHADO, Maria Helena. *Reprodução humana assistida*: aspectos éticos e jurídicos. 1. ed. (2003), 6ª tir. Curitiba: Juruá, 2008, p. 126.

9 In the words of Vera Lucia Raposo, for whom "the fertilization of an excessive number of oocytes is responsible for the creation of more embryos than can be transported to the maternal uterus under conditions which will enable the successful pregnancy without harming the life of the mother". RAPOSO, Vera Lúcia. "O dilema do rei Salomão: conflitos de vontade quando ao destino dos embriões excedentários", cit., p. 58.

10 The question is also found in U.S. doctrine: "Many states have not yet addressed issues involving embryo donation. (...) They may treat embryo donation like other forms of assisted reproduction, or they may have developed entirely new statutes reflecting the popular belief that there is something different about embryos compared to eggs and sperm alone". CAHN, Naomi R. *Test tube families*: why the fertility market needs regulation. New York/London: New York University Press, 2009, p. 96.

A basic question then erupts: when a aggregate of molecules ceases to be a simple chemical mixture and turns into a living organism?[11] There are two main currents in this regard.[12]

On one hand, some argue that human life has its beginning from fecundation. In this sense, there are authors that manifest themselves in order to understand that choosing a stage to say that from there the "entanglement of molecules" becomes a human being and begins to exist, would be a scientific falsehood, a fiction. Thus, proponents of this theory assert that the embryo should be considered a human being since the fecundation.[13]

In the opposing current is the theory of pre-embryo, which starts took place with the famous Report Warnock on Fertilization and Embryology, published in 1984 in the United Kingdom, where it is stated that before the 14th day of development, the zygote does not have a system central nervous and would be merely a "mass of cells". This orientation is followed by several states, including Brazil,

---

11 This question arises on all sides of the world. In this sense, the spanish Professor Alvarez-Diaz states that "*los extremos de la vida humana tienen un problema fundamental, tanto en lo ético como en lo jurídico: establecer el límite preciso entre gametos y un ser humano nuevo, así como el de un ser humano vivo a uno muerto: en ninguno de ambos casos resulta sencillo*". ÁLVAREZ-DÍAZ, Jorge Alberto. "El estatus biológico del embrión humano. El quimerismo interespecies como nuevo problema bioético y biojurídico", em Los avances del Derecho ante los Avances de la Medicina/ Salomé Adroher Biosca; Federico de Montalvo Jääskeläinen (Directores); María Reyes Corripio Gil-Delgado; Abel B. Veiga Copo (Coordinadores). Madrid: Thomson Aranzadi, pp. 977-990, 2008, p. 977.

12 "*Conceptionist*" and "*Natalist*". There is a current with a smaller number of supporters, called theory of conditional personality. About this last, Arnoldo Wald affirms that the unborn child is not subject of rights, although it deserves legal protection, both in civil and criminal level. The protection of the unborn can be explained because in it there is a conditional personality that comes in its fullness, with live birth and is extinguished in the case of the fetus´ death. WALD, Arnoldo. *Curso de Direito Civil Brasileiro*. Direito Civil Introdução e Parte Geral. 9. ed. São Paulo: Saraiva, 2002, p. 118.

13 See, for all SIQUEIRA, Marília de. "O início da vida e a Medicina atual", em *A vida dos direitos humanos*: Bioética médica e jurídica/ Ricardo Henry Marques Dip (org.). Porto Alegre: Sergio Fabris, p. 335-353, 1998, p. 338 e ss.

which on the CFM Resolution 1.358/92 adhered to this theory.[14] The same idea seems to have been adopted by Law 14/2007 of 3 July on Biomedical Research in Spain. The art. 3 require that the pre-embryo is an embryo formed in vitro consisting of the group of cells resulting from the progressive division of the oocyte, which is fertilized until 14 days later.[15]

Notwithstanding the existence of different currents on the legal status of the embryo we will pass off the discussion, not adhering to the "concepcionist" theory, to the theory of conditional personality or the "natalist" theory, nor will be treated the issue of the embryo constitute or not a natural person.[16]

---

14 Cf. KRELL, Olga Jubert Gouveia. *Reprodução Humana Assistida e Filiação Civil*: Princípios Éticos e Jurídicos. Curitiba: Juruá, 2006, p. 125.

15 The doctrine criticizes the law by, have differentiated the concept of pre-embryo and embryo and in the end, having named the pre-embryo, embryo, which made its understanding confused. Íñigo Beriain states that "(...) *si seguimos literalmente lo allí dicho, un preembrión que se encuentra en una placa de Petri nunca podrá ser un embrión, porque ni la organogénesis ha tenido lugar, ni, por supuesto, se halla en el útero de una mujer. Y, sin embargo, la definición de «preembrión» apunta justamente lo contrario cuando dice que un preembrión es un embrión o, para ser exactos, es el nombre que se le da a un embrión en los primeros catorce días de su vida, siempre que éste haya sido constituído in vitro*". BERIAIN, Íñigo de Miguel. "El concepto de embrión en la Ley 14/2007, de 3 de julio, de investigación biomédica", em Los avances del Derecho ante los Avances de la Medicina/ Salomé Adroher Biosca; Federico de Montalvo Jääskeläinen (Directores); María Reyes Corripio Gil-Delgado; Abel B. Veiga Copo (Coordinadores). Madrid: Thomson Aranzadi, pp. 991-1005, 2008, p. 993.

16 About the legal status of the unborn and the various existing currents, see PAMPLONA FILHO, Rodolfo; ARAÚJO, Ana Thereza Meirelles de. "Tutela Jurídica do Nascituro à Luz da Constituição Federal" em *Revista Magister de Direito Civil e Processual Civil*. v. 18, Maio/Junho: Porto Alegre: Magister, pp. 35-48, 2007, pp. 37-40.

What is really at issue is determining whether the embryo is a thing (*res*),[17] a quasi-property,[18] a human being,[19] a potential human being,[20] or a tertium genus,[21] a category of rights and relations, yet unnamed. Following the idea of Vera Lucia Raposo, the latter view appears to be most reasonable to adopt.[22]

Under a rigorous legal definition of a person, an embryo – or pre-embryo, cannot be considered a person. However, they also do not fit on a definition of property, because you cannot dispose them in any and every situation, and neither party has exclusive rights over them. This conclusion shows that when it comes to embryos, the legal rights are not exact. Thus, it can be stated that the embryos find themselves somewhere in between the two definitions.[23]

---

17 This is the opinion of CAHN, Naomi R. *Test tube families*, cit., p. 175, when she states that despite the embryos are recipients of special respect, they still constitute property, such as sperm and eggs.

18 Property for certain purposes, but not all, according to GARRISON. "Law Making for Baby Making: An Interpretive Approach to the Determination of Legal Parentage", em *Harvard Law Review* 113, pp. 835 e ss., 2000, p. 906.

19 In this current is affiliated Enrique Varsi Rospigliosi, for whom the embryo, even *ex utero* is a human life that, regardless of how it was created and if it is waiting to be transferred to the uterine wall, deserves legal protection as a subject of rights as it is. In this sense, see ROSPIGLIOSI, Enrique Varsi. *Derecho genético y procreático*. 4ª ed. atual. 1ª ed. para Bolívia. La Paz: ABIODGE – Asociación Boliviana de Bioética & Derecho Genético y Biotecnología, 2005, p. 125.

20 Cf. DELGADO, Mário Luiz. "Reprodução assistida: a nova resolução do Conselho Federal de Medicina e o descarte de embriões. Questão ética ou legal?", em *Jus Navigandi*, Teresina, ano 16, n. 2774, 4 fev. 2011. Available in: <http://jus.uol.com.br/revista/texto/18410>. Access on: 26/04/2011. Similarly, considers the embryo a potential human being – and, therefore is opposed to the experiments that will lead to its destruction: MARSHALL, John. "The Case Against Experimentation", em *Experiments on Embryos*/ A. Dyson; J. Harris (editors). London: Routledge, pp. 55-64, 1990, p. 55.

21 Latin expression that designates halfway between two things. In the present case, the embryos would be somewhere between the things and human beings.

22 Cf. RAPOSO, Vera Lúcia. "O dilema do rei Salomão: conflitos de vontade quando ao destino dos embriões excedentários", cit., p. 57.

23 In the same sense, see ERICKSON, Thereza M.; ERICKSON, Megan T. "What happens to embryos when a marriage dissolves? Embryo disposition and divorce", em *William Mitchell Law Review*, vol. 35, Issue 2, pp. 469- 488, 2009, p. 481.

So we need to see the surplus embryo in a kind of hybrid theory, where it does not fit the figure of person, "but is recipient of rights aimed at curbing excessive and unethical practices the scientific world".[24] [25] Regardless of the view that one has about the legal nature of the embryo, an idea must be taken for granted: there is an almost general consensus that they deserve a "special respect" because they have completed the first steps after fertilization to become a baby.[26]

5. Who has the power to dispose the surplus embryos?

At a first moment, one must question whether we should speak of "custody" of embryos – in a clear reference to parental rights – departing from an idea that embryos constitute human life, albeit in a distinct form from the human being born, or if we should speak of property or possession, a clear qualification of the embryos as mere *res*.[27]

Irrespective of the qualification that is given to the embryo – of thing or human being – a certainty must exist. Prior to the time of realization of IVF, or at most, until the moment of the embryo cryopreservation, its destination must be – or should be – provided in a

24 Cf. SOARES, Vladimir Salles. "O embrião excedentário e as terapias celulares – uma análise da lei de biossegurança sob o prisma constitucional", em *Novos direitos*/ Mauro Nicolau Júnior. Curitiba: Juruá, pp. 625-691, 2007, p. 658.

25 Notwithstanding the idea has not been adopted in the trial Davis *v.* Davis, this current already was ventilated: "A *third view -- one that is most widely held -- takes an intermediate position between the other two. It holds that the pre-embryo deserves respect greater than that accorded to human tissue but not the respect accorded to actual persons. The pre-embryo is due greater respect than other human tissue because of its potential to become a person and because of its symbolic meaning for many people. Yet, it should not be treated as a person, because it has not yet developed the features of personhood, is not yet established as developmentally individual, and may never realize its biologic potential*". *Davis v. Davis,* 842 S.W. 2d 588 (Tennessee, 1992), [57].

26 Two decades ago manifested this idea ROBERTSON, John apud GARRISON. "Law Making for Baby Making: An Interpretative Approach to the Determination of Legal Parentage", cit., p. 910.

27 This question is also raised by RAPOSO, Vera Lúcia. "Direitos reprodutivos", cit., p. 129.

contract or in the informed consent used by the clinic, since otherwise, many problems may arise, particularly in the event of separation of the couple or death of one of them.

Moreover, the resolution of CFM 2.121/2015 expressly states that at the time of cryopreservation, spouses or partners should express their willingness in writing as to the destination that will be given to pre-embryos cryopreserved in the event of divorce, serious illness or death of one or both, and when they wish to donate them.

The solution, in theory, seems to have been offered: what is in the contract or in the informed consent form is valid to decide the destination of excess embryos. And the parents – biological and "socio-affective" – will decide the issue.

And what the absence of a written document? What could happen? And if the consent was not sufficiently clear? And if happens a disagreement between the beneficiaries? *Quid faciendum*? What will be the solution?

And once again we return to the problem of determining whether the embryos should be considered human beings, and conflicts resolved as is solved the assignment of custody of an infant; if they should be considered property and the disagreement be resolved as if the embryo constitute a mere thing, or, a third possibility, if the case should be viewed as a conflict of rights, specifically a conflict of reproductive rights, as asserts Vera Lúcia Raposo.[28]/[29] The jurist also states that the recipients of could invoke a "decisive power" over the embryos substantiated by a duty of care, from which emerge obligations to protect, but also rights.[30]

---

28 RAPOSO, Vera Lúcia. "O dilema do rei Salomão: conflitos de vontade quando ao destino dos embriões excedentários", cit., p. 56.

29 The same question is brought by the U.S. doctrine when it states that there is only a handful of cases – often without binding precedent – that are available to assist the court system to determine if the disposition of embryos should be analyzed under the scope of the law of contracts or as a constitutional right to have or not have children, which is defined as freedom of procreation. In this sense, see ERICKSON, Thereza M.; ERICKSON, Megan T. "What happens to embryos when a marriage dissolves? Embryo disposition and divorce", cit., p. 475.

30 Before reaching this conclusion, the legal expert brings to light a case that occurred in Brazil over a dispute in relation to an animal, namely a dog that,

In the event of biological parents being in harmony about the destination of embryos and, obviously, that destination is lawful, does not seem to exist problems on the matter. However, if the couple is in disagreement, the resolution of the situation should be left to another authority, preferably judicial and be based on what is meant by the best interest of the embryo.[31] And this disagreement can manifest itself in various ways. Both parents may want the embryos to procreate. One may want to deploy them and the other part opposes to engage into a parental project.

So, once again, it is imperative to reinforce the necessity of elaboration of a written agreement,[32] where such situations – of destination of the embryos – have already been decided at the outset, clarified the terms under which it will operate the uterine transfer in the event of separation or divorce.[33]

U.S. decisions oscillate between configuring decision-making power of dispose of embryos on the grounds of contract law or as a constitutional right to have or not have children. When American courts use the concepts of constitutional law as a way to decide these cases, as a rule, they have decided in favor of the part that is trying to avoid procreation.[34]

An example is the emblematic case Davis *v.* Davis. In the final decision of the Supreme Court of Tennessee, it was determined that disputes involving the disposition of pre-embryos produced by

"found in a conceptual limbo, somewhere between the people and things." Thusshe qualifies them as a tertium genus and states that "the embryos find themselves more or less at this point: such as the animals are living beings, but not people," and poses the question: "can the *tertium genus*, for some purposes at least, be treated as persons? The answer that the Brazilian doctrine offered was of an alleged duty of care towards animals, foundation of rights over them and, concomitantly, of duties". RAPOSO, Vera Lúcia. "O dilema do rei Salomão: conflitos de vontade quando ao destino dos embriões excedentários", cit., p. 56.

31 Cf. RAPOSO, Vera Lúcia. "O dilema do rei Salomão: conflitos de vontade quando ao destino dos embriões excedentários", cit., p. 61.

32 The disposition agreement.

33 In the same way, see RAPOSO, Vera Lúcia. "O dilema do rei Salomão: conflitos de vontade quando ao destino dos embriões excedentários", cit., p. 63.

34 ERICKSON, Thereza M.; ERICKSON, Megan T. "What happens to embryos when a marriage dissolves? Embryo disposition and divorce", cit., p. 476.

IVF should be resolved first, taking into account the preferences of the parents. If their wishes could not be determined, or if there was disagreement, then the prior agreement on disposition of embryos should be respected. If there was no prior agreement, the parties' interests in using or not pre-embryos should be considered. The Court asserted that usually the party who wished to avoid procreation should have prevalence, assuming that the other party would have a reasonable chance of achieving parenthood by other means than the use of pre-embryos in question (such as adoption, for example). If there were no reasonable alternatives, then the argument for the use of pre-embryos to achieve pregnancy should be considered. However, if the party that demanded control of pre-embryos only wanted to donate them to another couple, the other party's interest in not having children, should prevail.[35]

Even though diverging of the court below that gave Mary Sue Davis the custody of the seven surplus embryos, the two courts departed from the same assumption, that embryos are not things subject to property law[36], but human beings whose destination should be resolved under the rules of parental rights.[37]

Differently, the New York Court of Appeals in 1998 reached its decision in the case Kass *v.* Kass,[38] invoking the law of contracts and execution of disposition agreements, instead of utilizing a constitutional analysis as in the case Davis.[39] The Court held that the agreement was fairly clear about the destination of the surplus embryos in addition to consider that it was too costly to the father be coerced

---

35 *Davis v. Davis*, 842 S.W. 2d 588 (Tennessee, 1992), [112].

36 "One of the fundamental issues the inquiry poses is whether the pre-embryos in this case should be considered "persons" or "property" in the contemplation of the law. The Court of Appeals held, correctly, that they cannot be considered "persons" under Tennessee law". *Davis v. Davis*, 842 S.W. 2d 588 (Tennessee, 1992), [45].

37 Cf. RAPOSO, Vera Lúcia. "O dilema do rei Salomão: conflitos de vontade quando ao destino dos embriões excedentários", cit., p. 67.

38 *Kass v. Kass*, 696 N.E.2d (N.Y. 1998).

39 Cf. ERICKSON, Thereza M.; ERICKSON, Megan T. "What happens to embryos when a marriage dissolves? Embryo disposition and divorce", cit., p. 477.

into an unwanted parenthood.[40] Thus, the Court gave the embryos to the clinic for scientific research.[41]

It is an evident fact that no one can predict the future, neither the couple nor the medical team involved in the process of assisted reproduction. Consider the situation that occurred in the case Roman *v.* Roman, USA. This case began in the state of Texas and ended up being decided in the Supreme Court of the United States. The only reason because husband's will prevailed and prevented that his ex-wife had the embryos implanted was the fact that he signed the informed consent form and specified the agreement about the disposition of embryos.[42]

Due to the analysis of cases and the doctrine on the matter, in relation to disputes between living parents desires, we align for the solution proposed by Vera Lucia Raposo, where the jurist says that you must choose a resolution based on the following considerations: 1) in case of disagreement among the beneficiaries of the techniques, should be applied the established in prior agreements between the parties, 2) in the absence of such agreements should be considered the relief of the will of each party to use or not the embryos, with a prevalence of the right to not reproduce, especially when the desire of the other party is in order to allocate the embryos to a third party, 3) however, if the man or woman that want to use the embryos do not have an alternative way to reproduce, the right of this individual to reproduce must have

---

40 Cf. RAPOSO, Vera Lúcia. "O dilema do rei Salomão: conflitos de vontade quando ao destino dos embriões excedentários", cit., p. 68.

41 "As they embarked on the IVF program, appellant and respondent--"husband" and "wife," signing as such--clearly contemplated the fulfillment of a life dream of having a child during their marriage. The consents they signed provided for other contingencies, most especially that in the present circumstances the pre-zygotes would be donated to the IVF program for approved research purposes. These parties having clearly manifested their intention, the law will honor it". *Kass v. Kass*, 696 N.E.2d (N.Y. 1998), [64].

42 Cf. ERICKSON, Theresa M. *Surrogacy and Embryo, Sperm & Egg Donation*: What Were You Thinking? Considering IVF & Third-Party Reproduction. New York: iUniverse, 2010, p. 162

prevalence, considering that the initial parental project was supported by both sides, even by that part that now opposes implantation.[43]

However, the solution proposed above fits in cases of dispute in life. What if in the case of death, in the absence of a written agreement?[44] Once more we return to the same question: are we talking about an asset that would be passed on by inheritance or testament, or would – automatically – the decision into the hands of the survivor, as with parental responsibilities?

One form of assisted reproduction post-mortem is the embryo transfer. In this modality, as a rule, there was consent of the male part, which authorized the use of their semen for the fertilization of eggs of the female element of the couple. However, such consent was given, usually with the intention that the process was completed during the life of the deceased. Thus it remains to be ascertained whether it would remain in the event that the individual know that would die soon and his child would be born only in later time.[45]

If we accept the transfer of embryos post-mortem, following the idea proposed by the doctrine should be followed two assumptions: 1) it is necessary that the husband or partner has left an express statement to allow it;[46] 2) The technique should be taken out within a specified period after the death of the deceased.[47]

In the absence of an agreement covering also the question of a possible post-mortem embryo transfer, the decisions can derail either

43 RAPOSO, Vera Lúcia. "O dilema do rei Salomão: conflitos de vontade quando ao destino dos embriões excedentários", cit., p. 78-79.

44 There is no guarantee that everything goes as agreed to go. In this sense, see the case A.Z. v. B.Z., 1051 N.E.2d 725 (Mass. 2000). Situation the Supreme Court of Massachusetts refused the accomplishment of the agreement.

45 See RAPOSO, Vera Lúcia; DANTAS, Eduardo. "Aspectos jurídicos da reprodução assistida *post-mortem*, em perspectiva comparada Brasil-Portugal", em *Lex Medicinae* – Revista Portuguesa de Direito da Saúde, ano 7, n. 14. Coimbra: Centro de Direito Biomédico/ Coimbra Editora, pp. 81-94, 2010, p. 83

46 This reasoning can be used not only in relation to the male deceased, but also in relation to the female element of the couple, provided that the legal system in question admits the use of surrogate motherhood.

47 In this way, see RAPOSO, Vera Lúcia; DANTAS, Eduardo. "Aspectos jurídicos da reprodução assistida *post-mortem*, em perspectiva comparada Brasil-Portugal", cit., p. 93. RAPOSO, Vera Lúcia. "Direitos reprodutivos", cit., p. 124.

way, as in Brazil, it is necessary a statement or express authorization of the deceased. Let us consider some situations in France as an illustration of what may occur in the absence of such a document.[48]

Due to the lack of consent by the deceased parent the Court de Grande Instance of Rennes,[49] objected to the transfer of embryos post-mortem. In another spin, demonstrating the heterogeneity of decisions relating to the matter, a decision by the Court of Angers[50], authorized the embryo transfer in an analogous situation, and allowing even the infant to be considered the son of the deceased and that he could adopt his surname.[51]

6. The destination of the surplus embryos

The majority of existing rules – in particular the European – seek to restrict the number of embryos generated by reducing it to the number necessary for the success of insemination. However there is no a mathematically exact rule that ensures success without producing any surplus embryos.[52]

This issue is undoubtedly controversial. A problem that can be divided in liberal and conservative positions. At least when it comes to potentially destroy the embryos, as in the case of disposal or in scientific experiments.[53] What is the destination that must be given to

---

48 Remembering that in Brazil hardly a favorable decision would occur in the absence of a prior authorization, since the resolution of the Federal Council of Medicine explicitly presents as a requirement the existence of such a document.

49 Decision of 30 June 1993, Court de Grande Instance of Rennes.

50 Decision of November 10, 1992, Court de Grande Instance d'Angers, Première Chambre.

51 Examples brought by RAPOSO, Vera Lúcia; DANTAS, Eduardo. "Aspectos jurídicos da reprodução assistida *post-mortem*, em perspectiva comparada Brasil-Portugal", cit., pp. 88-90.

52 As states RAPOSO, Vera Lúcia. "Direitos reprodutivos", cit., p. 128.

53 The English doctrine states that any embryo used in research will be destroyed or perish. In this regard, cf. JACKSON, Emily. *Medical Law* – Text, Cases and Materials. 2nd edition. Oxford: Oxford University Press, 2010, p. 622. In contrast, Guilherme de Oliveira says that "in a broad concept of (scientific) research will fit non-destructive and destructive research or experimentation." Points as examples of non-destructive research the mere observations and the

the surplus embryos? Must be maintained for use by couples of origin or another couple? They must be destroyed, cryopreserved indefinitely or used for purposes of scientific research? How alert the Portuguese jurist Jorge Duarte Pinheiro, "the solution is open, because it depends on status that is recognized or granted to the human embryo."[54]

It is imperative to emphasize that the spirit of the Brazilian Constitution is undoubtedly favorable to the right to life, which is, strictly, the first, most basic and important of all fundamental human rights.[55] Within this logic, some issues may be raised: this fundamental right to life is autonomous?[56] Is it absolute? Some say yes[57], some say no.[58] Either way, we believe that any other destination other than the adoption of embryos – that is, their experimentation or their simple

---

"mild non-injurious interventions". OLIVEIRA, Guilherme de. "Um caso de selecção de embriões", em *Temas de Direito da Medicina*. 2ª ed. aum. Coimbra: Coimbra Editora, pp. 277-288, 2005, p. 279 e note 2.

54 PINHEIRO, Jorge Duarte. *O Direito da Família Contemporâneo*. Lisboa: AAFDL, 2008, p. 250.

55 The Brazilian Civil Code provides in its article 2, that "the civil personality of the person's begins with the birth with life, but the law puts on safe, from conception, the rights of the unborn." The emphasis of the issue is in the conception. The article cited seems to be based on the "conceptionist" theory that considers the beginning of life as a mere junction between sperm and egg (fecundation), in opposition to the theory adopted by Resolution of the Federal Council of Medicine.

56 It seems that in the absence of parental consent, in the long term, when is characterized an "abandonment" of these embryos, the clinic or competent authority that may dispose of them, shall, in a foreground try a parental project with third parties, and in the failure of this attempt move to the alternatives, in a idea of prevalence – but not absolutism – of the right to life.

57 For Ives Gandra Martins, the Brazilian Constitution protects the life of any human being, even though "imperfect" or subject to limitations, which translates into a guarantee of life "without qualitative". MARTINS, Ives Granda da Silva. "O Direito Constitucional comparado e a inviolabilidade da vida humana", em A vida dos direitos humanos: Bioética médica e jurídica/ Ricardo Henry Marques Dip (org.). Porto Alegre: Sergio Fabris, p. 127-144, 1998, p. 137.

58 See, for all KUHSE, Helga, SINGER, Peter. "Individuals, Humans and Persons: The Issue of Moral Status," in Embryo Experimentation / Peter Singer et al. (editors). Cambridge: CUP, p. 65-75, 1990, where the authors defend that not only the right to life is not absolute, as that experimentation on human embryos should be allowed even if the embryo is considered a person.

destruction – should be subsidiary. One should always keep in mind the solution that most dignifies and protects the embryo in question.

A "novelty" of Resolution 1.957/2010, repeated in the current Resolution of the Federal Council of Medicine has caused some stir in the doctrine.[59] The express possibility of disposal of surplus embryos considered nonviable. On the issue asserts Mario Delgado that the resolution of CFM, by allowing the "disposal" of embryos, violates the fundamental right to life. Especially because it does not establish clear and objective requirements to identify which embryos should be considered "viable" and therefore subject to "dump". According to the jurist, the decision may derail into arbitrariness, leaving up to each clinic or each professional the decision about the viability of a life of a human being.[60]

It is certain that the destruction – pure and simple – of embryos is one of the issues that bring the most controversy and debate within the techniques of assisted reproduction. On grounds of all kinds: scientific, moral, philosophical. The claim of the inviolable right to life is perfectly understandable. However the claim of lack of objective requirements to identify non-viable embryos does not seem reasonable. Consider this:

Decree n. 5591 of 22 November 2005 establishes in its Article 3, XIII that should be considered non-viable embryos "those with genetic alterations evidenced by pre implantation diagnosis, according to specific standards established by Ministry of Health, which had their development interrupted by lack spontaneous cleavage after a period exceeding twenty-four hours from IVF, or morphological alterations that compromise the full development of the embryo". We will refrain from discussing other issues, such as issues relating to pre implantation diagnosis, for example. The truth is that guidelines and objective

---

59 Is placed in quotes because despite the CFM Resolution 1.358/92 expressly determine that surplus embryos should be cryopreserved in practice, is of public knowledge that some fertility clinics discarded the surplus embryos after the transfer of those selected to the uterus of the woman. In this way see Neste sentido, consultar PROPATO, Valéria. "Fábrica de gente", em *Revista Isto É*, n. 1679, pp. 86-90, 5 dez. 2001, p. 86 e ss.

60 DELGADO, Mário Luiz. "Reprodução assistida: a nova resolução do Conselho Federal de Medicina e o descarte de embriões. Questão ética ou legal?", cit.

criteria about what constitutes a viable embryo there are. If they are reasonable or ethical is another question. Pondering between an *ad eternum* freezing as required under the previous resolution and disposal as proposed by the resolution into effect is a very ungrateful task.

It seems that neither a solution nor the other seem to be reasonable enough. Once considered unviable to lead a pregnancy to term, does not mean that all embryos will be useless for any experimentation, reason why would a better idea that the resolution had determined that such embryos – since they are not in conditions of being deployed – would cryopreserved for the purpose of research and not directly discarded.

One issue that is equally or more disturbing than the determination of the viability of the embryo is the time criterion presented by the Brazilian Biosafety Law for the cryopreserved embryos to be used in experiments. Such criteria does not seem to possess an objectivity that justifies it. This is because the embryos can be frozen for decades and still be viable to carry out a pregnancy.[61]

There has been news that babies came from embryos frozen for eight years (Brazil), 13 (Spain) or until almost 20 years (USA).[62] Specialists in assisted reproduction techniques such as Richard Fleming, of the Centre for Reproductive Medicine, University of Glasgow, claim that cases like these demonstrates how an embryo of good quality (so-called, viable) can perfectly develop independent of having been generated in 1990 or 20 years later.[63]

---

61 In contrast: "The embryos of five or more years of cryopreservation, and some before, are almost all dying, unfit for intrauterine transfer (Statement of Vote of the Counselor Daniel Serrão Opinion n. 44/CNECV/04)". RAPOSO, Vera Lúcia. "O dilema do rei Salomão: conflitos de vontade quando ao destino dos embriões excedentários", cit., p. 56

62 Five embryos that had been donated anonymously by a couple about 20 years earlier were defrosted. Two of them survived and were transferred to the uterus of the patient, at the end of a single pregnancy, gave birth to a healthy boy. The case was reported in a scientific paper in the journal Fertility and Sterility, of the American Society for Reproductive Medicine. Cf. "Bebê nasce de embrião congelado há quase 20 anos". Available in: http://www.bbc.co.uk/portuguese/ciencia/2010/10/101011_embriao_congelado_pu.shtml Access on: 15/12/2011.

63 Cf. "Bebê nasce de embrião congelado há quase 20 anos", cit.

Based on these examples, not as uncommon as one might think, can be questioned: it is reasonable the deadline set by the legislation in question? There are objective factors that have established it or was merely a temporary appointment in order not to let such a task to be resolved casuistically and stand at the mercy of some arbitrary? Another question not easy to answer. Certainly the embryos cannot be cryopreserved ad infinitum. But given the examples above, the period of three years determined by the Brazilian Biosafety Law does not seem to offer us an objective and reasonable criteria.

Perhaps such time limit is based on the idea being to prevent an infinite storage, in order to avoid situations like the U.S. that have now, somewhere around 500,000 viable embryos cryopreserved. Assuming that cryopreservation has no fixed period in the country, one can assume that many others thousands – unviable – can be frozen in U.S. territory. At another spin, the deadline for Brazil, by the advances that science has shown in recent times could be lengthened to somewhere between three years of now and the 20 years, since experts state that the embryo can still keep their viability.

6.1. A solution for now: adoption

It seems that it is already clear our position about the ideal destination for supernumerary embryos. Adoption. While it is not given primacy to the techniques of freezing eggs and surplus embryos continues to exist, this should be the "Plan A" for leftover embryos.

When confirmed the viability of an embryo, there is no reason that it is driven for use in research and, ultimately, destroyed, before any attempts to get it a parental project are exhausted. Therefore, although the situation is sui generis, it seems better to speak of adoption, than in donation since the primary purpose is to seek a family for these possible human beings.

Note that the solution in question is not about an encouragement to the production of embryos so that they can be "adopted". No. It is imperative to state that scientists and doctors must be cautious and act with restraint in obtaining the amount of eggs and in order not to obtain more embryos than are needed to achieve a reasonably successful deployment. The ideal is that all embryos produced were transferred to the patient. In the event of surpluses, it is preferable, however, that they are used in single women[64] or in other couples, including homosexuals.

Adoption[65] should always be preferred. In case of disagreement between the parents, whose impasse refers the matter to court, the destruction of embryos should always be a last resort. Notwithstanding the freedom and autonomy of the parties, is to understand that the search for implementation in other couples should be the first option.[66] In the absence of those who "adopt" an embryo may, then, give it another destination. The right to life of the human being in potential – although not absolute – must have some prevalence. Moreover, in the impossibility of a parental project, why not use aimed at the common benefit in opposition to the destruction pure and simple?

6.2. A solution for the future: the freezing of gametes

For some time now the doctrine – including the favorable to scientific experimentation on embryos – manifested in the sense of the necessity of the technique of IVF to be regulated so that it occasioned a minimum of spare embryos, at the risk of perpetuate the situation of cryopreservation of the embryos or simply discarding.[67]

As previously mentioned, the technique of egg freezing was for a long time inadequate to provide a safe storage of eggs. However, as with almost everything in the medical field, this issue has also evolved and a "plan B", if not a master plan emerged to avoid the creation of new embryos: the freezing of eggs. It is known that the number of

---

64 Or even a parental project of a single man, whose legal system permits use of surrogate motherhood.

65 Or donation, as the provision in question establishes.

66 About question, affirms Vera Lucia Raposo that the most desirable destination of these embryos is their donation to an infertile couple, allowing not only the preservation the life of the embryo, but also promoting the formation of a new family. RAPOSO, Vera Lúcia. "O dilema do rei Salomão: conflitos de vontade quando ao destino dos embriões excedentários", cit., p. 61.

67 In this regard see SOARES, Vladimir Salles. "O embrião excedentário e as terapias celulares – uma análise da lei de biossegurança sob o prisma constitucional", cit., p. 656.

surplus embryos in Brazil has grown and stopped because egg freezing is considered not only an alternative exit, but is a tendency.[68]

7. Conclusion

Some talk about adoption, others in donation. The embryo is seen as a property. The embryo is considered a person. We admit that the embryo is neither person nor a mere *res*, but *tertium genus*, a category of rights and relations, yet unnamed. Thus, in the case of destination of the embryos to another couple, it is better to talk about adoption, even if it is a species quite sui generis. At the end of the day, it is clear that the status of the embryo continues to be a gray area within the legal field.

We're not positioning ourselves against embryonic stem cell research, experiments on embryos, especially unviable. However like everything in life, particularly in science, there exists an evolution. In the specific case of IVF the solution of the problem of surplus embryos seems to be the freezing of gametes, namely, the cryopreservation of eggs that, over time, should lead to a reduction – in the medium term – and disappearance – in the long term – of the excess embryos. And with them will be taken many complex problems.

Many would argue that research on embryonic stem cells is necessary for the advancement of science. We have no doubt about it. But front of all of the above, it is clear our position that experimentation on human embryos should have a subsidiary nature. In other words: without any other option to develop this potential life it could be devoted to science. Starting to exist a "plan B" with an effective and efficient procedure of egg freezing that begins to prevent the creation of surplus embryos, the existence of the excess would characterize an arbitrary instrumentalization of them, violating their dignity. While this process was not possible, the existence of surplus embryo was justifiable. Not anymore.

However, while the supernumerary embryos continue to exist, its destination must be defined. One aspect – very important – often

68 Cf. PINTO, Angela Joenck. "Embriões congelados ficam sem destino;Brasil tem 8 mil", cit.

neglected in matters of cryopreservation is to prepare a thorough and complete agreement with the clinic, which determines all possible questions arising from the relation to the clinic and between the parties. The aforementioned agreement shall contain – among other things – the cost of preservation of embryos; the duration of cryopreservation; who might dispose of the embryos (especially in case of death or divorce); the preference between adoption by another couple or use in the experiments of the viable embryos after a certain period of time; preference between the cryopreservation for purpose of experiments or mere disposal of the non-viable embryos. A thorough and comprehensive agreement can prevent that many cases will go to court.

This fact proves to be so important that there is an indication or at least guidance on the need of drawing up the contract in the resolution of CFM. A very brief analysis of American jurisprudence shows us how the mere writing of a document can avoid a very complex dispute, which deals not only with personal rights of those involved in the process of assisted reproduction, but with the rights of the result of it: the beings that potentially are to come.

8. References

ÁLVAREZ-DÍAZ, Jorge Alberto. "El estatus biológico del embrión humano. El quimerismo interespecies como nuevo problema bioético y biojurídico", em *Los avances del Derecho ante los Avances de la Medicina*/ Salomé Adroher Biosca; Federico de Montalvo Jääskeläinen (Directores); María Reyes Corripio Gil-Delgado; Abel B. Veiga Copo (Coordinadores). Madrid: Thomson Aranzadi, pp. 977-990, 2008.

"Bebê nasce de embrião congelado há quase 20 anos". Disponível em: http://www.bbc.co.uk/portuguese/ciencia/2010/10/101011_embriao_congelado_pu.shtml Acesso em: 15/04/2011.

BERIAIN, Íñigo de Miguel. "El concepto de embrión en la Ley 14/2007, de 3 de julio, de investigación biomédica", em *Los avances del Derecho ante los Avances de la Medicina*/ Salomé Adroher Biosca; Federico de Montalvo Jääskeläinen (Directores); María Reyes Corripio Gil-Delgado; Abel B. Veiga Copo (Coordinadores). Madrid: Thomson Aranzadi, pp. 991-1005, 2008.

CAHN, Naomi R. *Test tube families:* why the fertility market needs regulation. New York/London: New York University Press, 2009.

CHAVES, Marianna. *Homoafetividade e Direito* – Proteção Constitucional, Uniões, Casamento e Parentalidade: Um Panorama Luso-Brasileiro. Curitiba: Juruá, 2011.

DANTAS, Eduardo; COLTRI, Marcos. *Comentários ao Código de Ética Médica*. Rio de Janeiro: Editora GZ, 2010.

DELGADO, Mário Luiz. "Reprodução assistida: a nova resolução do Conselho Federal de Medicina e o descarte de embriões. Questão ética ou legal?", em *Jus Navigandi*, Teresina, ano 16, n. 2774, 4 fev. 2011. Disponível em: <http://jus.uol.com.br/revista/texto/18410>. Acesso em: 26/04/2011.

ERICKSON, Theresa M. *Surrogacy and Embryo, Sperm & Egg Donation*: What Were You Thinking? Considering IVF & Third-Party Reproduction. New York: iUniverse, 2010.

______; ERICKSON, Megan T. "What happens to embryos when a marriage dissolves? Embryo disposition and divorce", em *William Mitchell Law Review*, vol. 35, Issue 2, pp. 469- 488, 2009.

GARRISON. "Law Making for Baby Making: An Interpretive Approach to the Determination of Legal Parentage," em *Harvard Law Review* 113, pp. 835 e ss., 2000.

GUIMARÃES, Ana Paula. *Alguns problemas jurídico-criminais da procriação medicamente assistida*. Coimbra: Coimbra Editora, 1999.

KRELL, Olga Jubert Gouveia. *Reprodução Humana Assistida e Filiação Civil*: Princípios Éticos e Jurídicos. Curitiba: Juruá, 2006.

KUHSE, Helga; SINGER, Peter. "Individuals, Humans and Persons: The Issue of Moral Status", em *Embryo Experimentation*/ Peter Singer *et al.* (editors). Cambridge: CUP, pp. 65-75, 1990.

JACKSON, Emily. *Medical Law* – Text, Cases and Materials. 2nd edition. Oxford: Oxford University Press, 2010.

MACHADO, Maria Helena. *Reprodução humana assistida*: aspectos éticos e jurídicos. 1. ed. (2003), 6ª tir. Curitiba: Juruá, 2008.

MARSHALL, John. "The Case Against Experimentation", em Experiments on Embryos/ A. Dyson; J. Harris (editors). London: Routledge, pp. 55-64, 1990.

MARTINS, Ives Granda da Silva. "O Direito Constitucional comparado e a inviolabilidade da vida humana", em *A vida dos direitos humanos*: Bioética médica e jurídica/ Ricardo Henry Marques Dip (org.). Porto Alegre: Sergio Fabris, p. 127-144, 1998.

OLIVEIRA, Guilherme de. "Um caso de selecção de embriões", em *Temas de Direito da Medicina*. 2ª ed. aum. Coimbra: Coimbra Editora, pp. 277-288, 2005.

OTERO, Paulo. *Personalidade e identidade pessoal e genética do ser humano*: um perfil constitucional da bioética. Coimbra: Almedina, 1999.

PAMPLONA FILHO, Rodolfo; ARAÚJO, Ana Thereza Meirelles de. "Tutela Jurídica do Nascituro à Luz da Constituição Federal" em *Revista Magister de Direito Civil e Processual Civil*. v. 18, Maio/ Junho: Porto Alegre: Magister, pp. 35-48, 2007.

PINHEIRO, Jorge Duarte. *O Direito da Família Contemporâneo*. Lisboa: AAFDL, 2008.

PINTO, Angela Joenck. "Embriões congelados ficam sem destino;Brasil tem 8 mil". Disponível em: http://noticias.terra.com.br/ciencia/noticias/0,,OI4890076-EI238,00-Embrioes+congelados+ficam+sem+destino+Brasil+tem+mil.html Acesso em: 05/04/2011.

PROPATO, Valéria. "Fábrica de gente", em *Revista Isto É*, n. 1679, pp. 86-90, 5 dez. 2001.

RAPOSO, Vera Lúcia. "Direitos reprodutivos", em *Lex Medicinae* – Revista Portuguesa de Direito da Saúde. Ano 2, n. 3. Coimbra: Centro de Direito Biomédico/ Coimbra Editora, pp. 111-131, 2005.

______. "O dilema do rei Salomão: conflitos de vontade quando ao destino dos embriões excedentários", em *Lex Medicinae* – Revista Portuguesa de Direito da Saúde. Ano 5, n. 9. Coimbra: Centro de Direito Biomédico/ Coimbra Editora, pp. 55-79, 2008.

______. "Pode trazer-me o menu, por favor? Quero escolher o meu embrião – os múltiplos casos de selecção de embriões em sede de diagnóstico genético pré-implantação", em *Lex Medicinae* – Revista Portuguesa de Direito da Saúde. Ano 4, n. 8. Coimbra: Centro de Direito Biomédico/Coimbra Editora, pp. 59-84, 2007.

______; DANTAS, Eduardo. "Aspectos jurídicos da reprodução assistida *post-mortem*, em perspectiva comparada Brasil-Portugal", em *Lex Medicinae* – Revista Portuguesa de Direito da Saúde, ano 7, n. 14. Coimbra: Centro de Direito Biomédico/ Coimbra Editora, pp. 81-94, 2010.

ROSPIGLIOSI, Enrique Varsi. *Derecho genético y procreático*. 4ª ed. atual. 1ª ed. para Bolívia. La Paz: ABIODGE – Asociación Boliviana de Bioética & Derecho Genético y Biotecnología, 2005.

SIQUEIRA, Marília de. "O início da vida e a Medicina atual", em *A vida dos direitos humanos*: Bioética médica e jurídica/ Ricardo Henry Marques Dip (org.). Porto Alegre: Sergio Fabris, p. 335-353, 1998.

SOARES, Vladimir Salles. "O embrião excedentário e as terapias celulares – uma análise da lei de biossegurança sob o prisma constitucional", em *Novos direitos*/ Mauro Nicolau Júnior. Curitiba: Juruá, pp. 625-691, 2007.

WALD, Arnoldo. *Curso de Direito Civil Brasileiro*. Direito Civil Introdução e Parte Geral. 9. ed. São Paulo: Saraiva, 2002.

WELTER, Belmiro Pedro. *Igualdade entre as filiações biológica e socioafetiva*. São Paulo: Editora Revista dos Tribunais, 2003.

11

TEST-TUBE FAMILIES: BRIEF REMARKS ON LEGAL LIMITS TO ART IN BRAZIL

Marianna Chaves

Summary: **1.** Introduction; **2.** The beneficiaries of ART in Brazil. **3.** Limits and exceptions. **4.** Surrogacy. **5.** Child-raising contracts. **6.** Conclusion. **7.** References.

1. Introduction

In a not-too-distant past, people or couples who were infertile or otherwise very difficult to procreate were doomed not to have children with whom they were genetically linked or simply to have no offspring. In the contemporary world this scenario has changed with the aid of reproductive technology that has substantially expanded the range of possibilities for procreation of infertile couples, single people or same-sex couples.

Infertility is a reality that has been present in the history of mankind since its earliest days. The Holy Bible has many examples of women affected by infertility, as Sarah (Abraham's wife) and Elizabeth (Mary's cousin). In the past, the concern about infertility was not focused on the recognition of the exercise of the fundamental right to parenthood by both spouses. On the contrary, it was linked to the social function of women, which was exclusively to generate and raise children. In the event of the impossibility of exercising this role, the woman was considered useless, stigmatized, ostracized and could even be repudiated (as still happens in some places today).[1]

---

1 See NEVES, M. Patrão. "PMA: do desejo de um filho ao filho desejado", In: *Separata de Do início ao fim da vida* – Actas do Colóquio de Bioética. Braga:

Thus, with the viability brought about by reproductive medicine and biotechnology, test-tube families or "ectogenetic"[2] families emerged. They are those familiar models with children from medically assisted procreation techniques. As Rodrigo da Cunha Pereira points out, reproductive techniques, coupled with juridical, psychoanalytic and philosophical discourse, have promoted ways for the foundation of new kinship bonds. The types may vary between homologous or heterologous processes depending on whether the genetic material belongs to both or only one or none of the members of the couple and also includes recourse to traditional or gestational surrogacy (depending on whether or not the egg belongs to the carrier mother).

As it is warned in the specialized doctrine, of all the matters currently under development in the Health Law, there are few so controversial and dynamic. This domain encompasses and reaches so many branches of law at the same time, and has such direct and profound consequences on people's lives. Its scientific potential, the ethical dilemmas generated by the dizzying progress of the techniques used in reproductive medicine, and the absence of previous legal parameters to solve controversies are some of the elements that, combined with the changes in the behavior and way of thinking of society, are establishing a new scenario of possibilities, alternatives and paths. Today's medicine allows embryos to be developed outside a woman´s body, to choose their phenotype and genotype characteristics, to freeze them, to implant them in women who will carry them for third parties, or even allow someone to have children many years after their death. How far can one go, or should one go?[3]

Regulations and legislation relating to procreation are likely to have significant constitutional implications, so efforts to regulate must deal with the nature of the right at stake. The Brazilian Constitution indicates that family planning should be based on the dignity of the human person and on responsible parenthood, and the State is

Faculdade de Filosofia da Universidade Católica Portuguesa, pp. 113-137, 2005, p. 115.

2 PEREIRA, Rodrigo da Cunha. *Dicionário de direito de família e sucessões*: ilustrado. São Paulo: Saraiva, 2015, p. 294.

3 These are questions raised by DANTAS, Eduardo. *Direito médico.* 3 ed. Rio de Janeiro: GZ, 2014, p. 289.

prohibited from any kind of control or interference in the exercise of this right. From this can be derived the understanding of a fundamental right to reproduction and consequent constitution of family.

Any territory that denies the right to parenthood to a part of the individuals, hindering their personal fulfillment violates their fundamental rights to equality and non-discrimination. It also obstructs the exercise of citizenship and puts in check the very democracy and dignity of people, by failing to promote positively and equally the fundamental freedoms of all its citizens. By way of comparison, the US Supreme Court, in several trials, recognized the right to procreate as a fundamental right, in a logic that States cannot compel a person to reproduce nor can they obstruct their ability to procreate. Thus, this right exists in a positive and negative sense.[4]

Some argue that these matters should be left to the decision of the parties, the members of the family, in the frame of the various "interim orders" – the ethics, ethics, the orientations of reflection committees. However, the dominant opinion in countries with a Roman-German matrix or the Civil Law system is in the sense of legislative intervention. Doctors and health professionals themselves – as appears from the explanatory memorandum of the CFM – call for legislation. Such a need may lie in the fact that physicians, biologists, and other health-related professionals are not satisfied with guidelines based solely on professional ethics or conviction, and aim for the law to determine with certainty what is and is not lawful. Unable to find themselves the boundaries of their art, at a time that expands the civil and criminal liability of medical acts, professionals possess knowledge that is not enough a "corporate ethics to legitimate scientific practice".[5]

Brazil, however, has left the regulation of the matter of medically assisted procreation in charge of medical deontology. It does not

4 See Cfr. SHIVAKUMAR, Pryianka. "Count Your Chickens before They Hatch – How Multiple Pregnancies Are Endangering the Right to Abortion", *In:*

5 As Guilherme de Oliveira points out in a text published before the emergence of the Law of Medically Assisted Procreation (Law 32/2006) in Portugal. OLIVEIRA, Guilherme de. "Aspectos jurídicos da procriação assistida", *In*: *Temas de Direito da Medicina*/ Guilherme de Oliveira. 2. ed. Coimbra: Coimbra Editora, pp. 5-30, 2005, p. 7.

seem to be the right decision. Incidentally, Resolutions 1.957/2010, 2.013/2013 and 2.121/2015 of the Federal Medical Council, in their explanatory statements indicate – expressly – the need to issue specific legislation and resemble the lethargy of the Legislature in fulfilling this obligation. Therefore, it is necessary for Brazil to advance and legislate in this area. Certainly, taking into account – or making a reference to – all the rules present and widely accepted in the CFM Resolution and protecting issues that were not foreseen, regulated in an inconsistent or incomplete way in the Resolution or in the current legislation.

The doctrine is categorical in the sense that a lack of legislative response in this matter ends may expose the parties to a high risk scenario, ruled by legal uncertainty and often by economic exploitation, due to the absence of regulation and sanctions to legal deviations.[6] In addition, it should be noted that Assisted Reproduction entails new dimensions of basic concepts such as motherhood and paternity, human dignity, monogamy, moral integrity, as well as raising new interpretations of classic legal rules or imposing new ones rules.

Therefore, it is not a matter that should be simply left to the deontology of medical professionals or to any other intermediate disciplines, to the free conscience of the people and the family or to the care of reflection committees. As Guilherme de Oliveira points out,[7] "it is a matter of State responsibility; is a matter of public interest that calls for legislative intervention". The Portuguese professor added "this need for intervention by the legislator was given by the Warnock and Benda commissions, respectively in England and Germany. The head of the British commission, Mary Warnock, in a brief commentary on the work she directed, said that there is agreement in society on one point: that legislation is necessary. In turn, the report ends with a list of recommendations that suppose or expressly require legislative intervention. The BENDA report also makes broad recommendations for legal intervention".

6 In this sense, see PREISLER, Andrea. "Assisted Reproductive Technology: The Dangers of an Unregulated Market and the Need for Reform", *In:*

7 See OLIVEIRA, Guilherme de. "Legislar sobre Procriação Assistida", cit., pp. 95-97.

The time is ripe to reconsider the right to procreate and assisted reproduction in a context of the 21st century. Thus, the present day reveals a suitable moment to re-energize the academic discussion about the meaning of the right to procreation in a "post-coital world".[8] Any study in this field must take into account the technological, social and academic changes in the last decades.

The present paper aims to deal with some specifically controversial points within the matter of medically assisted procreation. We have tried to highlight the urgent need for the enactment of specific legislation, as well as the inevitability of harmonizing existing norms in the legal system with the realities created by ART. As foreign doctrine warns, the history of the (lack of) regulation of ART highlights the phenomenon that strong public acceptance and market forces entrenched around new technologies often result in sub-optimal safety standards.[9]

2. The beneficiaries of ART in Brazil

Resolution no. 2.121 / 2015 of the Federal Council of Medicine determines that all capable persons who have sought the procedure and whose indication does not deviate from the limits of the resolution may be beneficiaries of the medically assisted procreation techniques. The parties must be fully in agreement and appropriately clarified, in accordance with the legislation in force. It is important to mention that it can only speak authentically of reproductive autonomy when there is an effective choice, based on correct and appropriate information.

It should be noted that informed consent and informed choice are not necessarily the same thing. In addition, Resolution 2.121 / 2015 began to use the terminology "free and informed consent" instead of "informed consent" contained in Resolution 2.013 / 2013. The current CFM Resolution states that, "informed consent will be mandatory for all patients undergoing assisted reproduction techniques. The medical aspects involving all the circumstances of the application of an RA technique will be explained in detail, as well as the results obtained

8 As states MUTCHERSON, Kimberly M. "Procreative pluralism", *In: Berkeley Journal of Gender, Law & Justice*, Vol. 30, n. 1, pp. 22-75, 2015, p. 24.

9 PREISLER, Andrea. "Assisted Reproductive Technology: The Dangers of an Unregulated Market and the Need for Reform", cit., p. 214.

in that treatment unit with the proposed technique. The information must also reach biological, legal and ethical data. The informed consent document shall be drawn up in a special form and shall be completed with the written agreement obtained from a bilateral discussion between the persons involved in the techniques of assisted reproduction".[10]

Not infrequently, people and couples are adequately informed, but tend to focus more on the advantages than on the dangers of PMA techniques. Throughout the process, it is imperative that the doctor does not condition patients even indirectly to make a decision; as such conduct would constitute oppression to the interest of deciding autonomously.[11] Only the informed choice fulfills the necessary requirements and leads to the completeness of the doctor's duty of information. On the subject, Eduardo Dantas[12] warns that to the patient, it is necessary to be in possession of all possible elements to understand it, so that – then yes – can exercise the faculty of consenting to the proposed treatment or intervention; choose another one of the existing alternatives, although less indicated by the professional that assists it; or even refuse to be treated. This procedure, which encompasses informed consent without being confused with it, is named informed choice.

These CFM´s ethical standards expressly states that the use of ART is authorized for single persons and homosexual couples, while the medical professional's right to conscientious objection is admitted. The Resolution also establishes that a shared gestation is allowed in the hypothesis of same-sex union between lesbians, when a partner or spouse will carry the fertilized embryo with the ovum of the other (a situation in which there is no occurrence of infertility or other medical issue that contraindicates the pregnancy).

Thus, it can be said that access to the techniques of PMA in Brazil is quite broad, and the use of reproductive medicine is open to heterosexual couples, single people, as well as female and

---

10 See CFM, Resolução 2.121/2015. Available online at: http://www.portalmedico.org.br/resolucoes/CFM/2015/2121_2015.pdf

11 See SILVESTRE, Margarida. *Embriões excedentários:* entre a técnica, a lei e a ética. Coimbra: Coimbra Editora, 2015, p. 61.

12 DANTAS, Eduardo. *Direito médico*, cit., p. 77.

male homosexual couples, with recourse to shared pregnancy and surrogacy. It could not be different, since the Federal Constitution protects the family, in any of its forms, having all the same dignity and consideration, and the Federal Supreme Court has recognized same-sex unions as family entities. In this logic, it is not excessive to affirm that Brazil consecrates a procreative pluralism,[13] supported by the idea of autonomy, equality and justice in reproduction.[14]

3. Limits and exceptions

The Federal Council of Medicine prohibits sexing or sex selection. According to Resolution 2.121/ 2015, medically assisted procreation techniques cannot be used to select sex (presence or absence of Y chromosome) or any other biological feature (such as eye color or hair structure) of future offspring, except in the case to prevent disease in the child that will be born.[15] That is, only in the case where the sex selection is carried out for medical reasons (as to avoid diseases or anomalies linked to one of the sex chromosomes) it will be authorized by the resolution. There are those who refer to the practice as "sexist eugenics".[16]

---

13 A society that recognizes pluralism in procreation reflects efforts to imagine and protect family pluralism as indicates MUTCHERSON, Kimberly M. "Procreative pluralism", cit., p. 27.

14 The reproductive justice movement aims to create a world where individuals have the economic, social and political power and resources to make healthy decisions about their bodies, sexuality and reproduction. See MUTCHERSON, Kimberly M. " ", *In:*

15 For example, in families with a history of X-linked diseases, such as Becker muscular dystrophy and Duchenne muscular dystrophy, sex determination provides a powerful tool for identifying male fetuses at risk for X-linked diseases, as states KING, Jaime S. "And Genetic Testing for All – The Coming Revolution in Non-Invasive Prenatal Genetic Testing", *In:*

16 REIS, Rafael Vale e. "Responsabilidade penal na procriação medicamente assistida – A criminalização do recurso à maternidade de substituição e outras opções legais duvidosas", *In: Lex Medicinae* – Revista Portuguesa de Direito da Saúde, Ano 7, n. 13, pp. 69-93, 2010, p. 79.

As Vera Lúcia Raposo[17] points out, most of the world's legislation on assisted reproduction prohibits sexing, except in the hypothesis of prevention of hereditary diseases connected to a particular sex. This is also the position of the Convention on Human Rights and Biomedicine (Article 14). Therefore, the choice of sex when there are no medical reasons or the choice of different characteristics of the sex enters the denomination of frivolous choices (color and structure of the hair, color of the eyes, IQ, type and physical vigor), a choice of characteristics that lead to the idea of a genetic refinement of the species.

The Resolution expressly prohibits the fecundation of human oocytes for any purpose other than human procreation. In this way, the creation of human embryos that are not intended for the procreation of the people involved in the reproductive process is strictly prohibited. In the case of multiple pregnancies (a relatively common occurrence in PMA processes), the CFM Resolution establishes a prohibition on the use of procedures and that aim at embryo reduction. The risks of multifetal pregnancy increase with each additional fetus. But even though the Resolution of the Federal Council of Medicine does not have the force of law, the embryonic reduction seems to be prohibited within the Brazilian legal system, since such practice would constitute the crime of abortion, under the terms of Article 124 of the Penal Code.

It should be noted that some time ago multiples pregnancy have been considered a true epidemic in the field of ART. To try to avoid this occurrence to the maximum, the CFM Resolution limits the number of ova and embryos to be transferred to the patient in a maximum of four, depending on the age. In the United States, it is estimated that between 30 and 35% of pregnancies among women using ART result in multiple children, resulting in risks for women and fetuses. Even if embryo or fetal reduction is allowed, it is important to note that the process means not only eliminating one or more developing fetuses, but it also puts the entire pregnancy at risk.

---

17 Cfr. RAPOSO, Vera Lúcia. "Pode trazer o menu, por favor? Quero escolher o meu embrião – Os múltiplos casos de selecção de embriões em sede de diagnóstico genético pré-implantação", *In: Lex Medicinae* – Revista Portuguesa de Direito da Saúde, Ano 4, n. 8, pp. 59-84, 2007, pp. 67-69.

On the other hand, in the hypothesis of no reduction in multifetal pregnancy, the patient and her children face other serious risks. Multiple pregnancies, including twins, create serious health risks for both mothers and their children. These women face greater risks of damaging conditions such as pre eclampsia, preterm birth and gestational diabetes. Mothers who carry multiple fetuses are also hospitalized frequently long before pregnancy reaches full term, have to endure prolonged rest and have higher rates of caesarean delivery. Thus, even if the embryonic or fetal reduction was authorized, the best medicine is directed towards always trying to avoid multiples pregnancy.[18]

The CFM Resolution still provides for the possibility of using pre-implantation genetic diagnosis (PIGD), which is one of the possible prenatal diagnoses. It is an alternative to classical prenatal diagnosis, with the peculiarity of having embryos existing outside the maternal womb. The resolution further states that in the event of verification of disease-causing genetic changes, embryos may be donated for research or discarded.

Genetic testing has created opportunities, but also dilemmas for use in private health care as well as in public health systems. Sequencing of the human genome and advances in areas such as genomics and bioinformatics has brought new diagnostic and therapeutic procedures. The US and some European countries have passed legislation on discrimination that genetic testing can cause. As genetic testing technologies advance, national and international guidelines attempt to prepare and educate health professionals to prescribe these tests and interpret their results.[19]

As Vera Lúcia Raposo warns, although it does not (yet) function as a safe guarantee for a healthy baby, it is certain that it is now possible to avoid a series of serious diseases. As an example of the various aneuploidies detectable by screening, a method that allows

18 In this sense, see GLENNON, Theresa. "Choosing One: Resolving the Epidemic of Multiples in Assisted Reproduction", *In: Villanova Law Review* , Vol. 55, n. 1, pp. 147-204, 2010, p. 147 e p. 158.

19 KATZ, Gregory; SCHWEITZER, Stuart O. "Implications of Genetic Testing for Health Policy", *In: Yale Journal of Health Policy, Law, and Ethics*, Vol. 10, n. 1, pp. 90-134, 2010, p. 92.

the analysis of the number of chromosomes (21, 18, 13, X and Y)[20] of the available embryos in order to use only those that do not present chromosomal alterations, in order to increase the success rate of the ART and simultaneously reduce the number of embryos implanted at each attempt.

It is important to emphasize that the DGPI does not arise without challenges and complications. Often doctors themselves do not fully understand the results of a genetic test, or are not well trained in communicating the findings to patients. In addition, while most existing genetic tests examine disorders and pathologies that arise from the mutation of a single gene, the vast majority of hereditary conditions and traits result from interactions of multiple genes or between genes and the environment.[21]

In Brazil – through Resolution 2.121 / 2015 – it is also allowed that ART are used for typing of the HLA system of the embryo. This mechanism has the objective of selecting HLA-compatible embryos with a child of the couple already affected by the disease and whose effective treatment is the transplantation of stem cells, according to the current legislation. It is the so-called – and controversial – savior sibling technique. This child will be created to be genetically compatible with a sibling who suffers from a serious pathology whose cure or treatment consists in a transplant of cells or organs that will only be possible through the person who will be born. Thus, the "remedy-baby" or "savior sibling" comes, as a rule, when a couple faces the imminent death of a child and desperately attempts to avoid the worst. Thus, they decide to have another child, with equal genetic heritage, whose tissues will be compatible with those of the sibling and will be transplanted with little or no risk of rejection.[22]

---

20 Down syndrome, that is, three chromosomes in the 21st pair; Patau's syndrome, trisomy 13; Edward syndrome, trisomy 18; Klinefelter syndrome, which presupposes the existence of two X chromosomes, creating the triad XXY; Syndrome of Turner, characterized by the inexistence of a sexual chromosome, which leaves the X chromosome alone.

21 In this sense, see KING, Jaime S. "And Genetic Testing for All – The Coming Revolution in Non-Invasive Prenatal Genetic Testing", cit.

22 See RAPOSO, Vera Lúcia. "Pode trazer o menu, por favor? Quero escolher o meu embrião – Os múltiplos casos de selecção de embriões em sede de diagnóstico genético pré-implantação", cit., p. 71.

4. Surrogacy

Certainly, the question of the legality of surrogacy contracts is one of the most fascinating and challenging issues, as well as problematic within Health and Family Law. CFM Resolution 2.121/2015 authorizes the use of surrogacy, in the event of any medical impediment or contraindication that the gestation is carried out by the genetic donor. It is also authorized in the case of same-sex unions.

Surrogates must belong to the family of one of the partners in kinship up to the fourth degree, and other cases are subject to the analysis and authorization of the respective Regional Council of Medicine. Therefore, the new Resolution has extended this possibility. Currently a person who is not family as long as it is expressly authorized by the CRM can help the intended parents. Temporary donation of the uterus, as well as the donation of gametes and embryos, according to the Resolution cannot be commercial or profitable, and donors should not know the recipients' identity and vice versa. From this statement and the fact that CFM establishes a kinship rule between the patients and the surrogate mother, it follows that the carrier mother can not (or should not be) the genetic mother of the child, and the embryos must have been Fertilized with anonymous donor egg.[23]

Resolution 2.121/2015 establishes that in ART centers, the following documents and observations should be included in the patient's medical records: a) Informed consent signed by patients and the temporary donor of the uterus, observing bio psychosocial dimensions and risks Included in the pregnancy-puerperal process, as well as juridical aspects of the filiation; b) Medical report with the psychological profiles, certifying clinical and emotional adjustment of all parties involved in the process; C) Commitment Agreement between the patients and the surrogate, establishing clearly the question of the filiation of the embryos; D) Guarantee, by patients contracting services of ART, of treatment and medical care, including

23 Thus, in theory, traditional surrogacy – where the mother is also an egg donor – would be a prohibited practice. For a more in-depth differentiation between surrogacy modalities BARON, Noah; BAZZELL, Jennifer. "Assisted Reproductive Technologies", *In*: *Georgetown Journal of Gender and the Law*, Vol. 15, n. 1, pp. 57-94, 2014, p. 59.

by multidisciplinary teams, if prescribed, to the surrogate until the puerperium; E) Guarantee of the civil registry of the child by the patients, and that this documentation will be prepared during the pregnancy; E) Authorization of the spouse or partner, submitted in writing, if the surrogate is married or lives in a stable union.

There are some authors who affirm that the Resolutions of the Federal Medical Council, in the face of legislative silence, would have a "mandatory-general binding"[24] character based on Art. 59 of Brazilian Constitution. However, the Resolutions indicated in Art. 59, VII of Constitution/88 are only intended to regulate matters of internal interest (administrative or political) of the Chamber of Deputies and the Federal Senate, jointly or separately. Therefore, it does not seem feasible for the CFM Resolution ART to have force of law, binding the parties or the judge who will settle a possible litigation.

However, this does not mean that in the judicial proceedings its principles and provisions cannot be taken into account in the decision. The Code of Civil Procedure establishes that the judge does not relinquish to sentence or dispatch by arguing a loophole or obscurity of the law. In the judgment of the dispute shall apply the legal rules; in the case of non-existence – as is the case – he will resort to analogy, customs and general principles of law. Also presents this reasoning the Article 4 of the Law of Introduction to the Norms of Brazilian Law.

With this outline and in the absence of specific legislation on ART, some questions can be posed: in the event of a free surrogacy contract, is contract valid? Could its binding force be upheld in the Resolution of the Federal Medical Council without any room for regret or breach in a logic of *pacta sunt servanda*? What about the event of an onerous contract? Would it immediately be considered null and void on the basis of CFM or infra-constitutional legislation? The answer does not appear to be absolutely clear and can go anywhere, depending on the views of the magistrate. The Brazilian civil law does not allow or prohibit surrogacy contracts (either free or commercial) unlike other systems.

Paragraph 4 of Article 199 of the Federal Constitution states that the law will prescribe conditions and requirements that facilitate the removal of organs, tissues and human substances for

---

24 DANTAS, Eduardo. *Direito médico*, cit., pp. 300-301.

the purpose of transplantation, research and treatment, as well as the collection, processing and transfusion of Blood and its derivatives, being prohibited any type of commercialization. The Magna Charta therefore refers to specific legislation. Thus, this article is one of those of limited effectiveness, since the applicability is dependent on infra-constitutional legislation.[25]

In the Brazilian legal system, Law n. 9.434/97 (Transplantation Law) provides for the removal of organs, tissues and parts of the human body for transplantation and treatment and other measures. But soon in its Article 1, it establishes that the free disposal of tissues, organs and parts of the human body, in life or post mortem, for the purpose of transplantation and treatment, is allowed. However, the next paragraph asserts that for the purposes of this law, blood, sperm and ovum are not included.

Law n. 11.105/2005 (Biosafety Law) establishes its Article 5, paragraph 3, prohibition of commercialization of the biological material referred to in this article and its practice implies the crime typified in Art. 15 of Law n. 9.434/97. This article expressly punishes the purchase or sale of tissues, organs or parts of the human body with imprisonment (from three to eight years) and a fine (200 to 360 days-fine). But the Transplant Law itself expressly warns that its rules do not apply to sperm and egg.

If the embryo/fetus is a result of the connection between sperm and ovum, is it covered or removed from the scope of the punishment contained in the legislation? This stormy question highlights the urgent and unassailable need for the creation of a specific law on ART to address these issues. The doctrine[26] is unanimous on the urgent need for legislative discipline of ART, in order to regulate the matter and avoid making mistaken exegesis of other legislations.

Depending on the interpretation given to these existing legal provisions, commercial surrogacy may be considered valid or not. If it

25 See SILVA, José Afonso da. *Comentário contextual à Constituição*, cit., p. 772.

26 NAMBA, Edison Tetsuzo. "Direito à identidade genética ou direito ao reconhecimento das origens e a reprodução assistida heteróloga", *In: Doutrinas essenciais* – Família e sucessões: direito de família/ Yussef Said Cahali; Francisco José Cahali (Orgs.). São Paulo: Editora Revista dos Tribunais, pp. 1385-1406, 2011, p. 1405.

is considered that the embryo/fetus would be included in the provisions of the aforementioned legislation, the contract shall be considered null and void, pursuant to clauses II and VII of Article 166 of the Civil Code. In the event of considering that the fetus / embryo would not be covered by the prohibition of Law n. 9.434/97, the contract may be considered valid, although morally reprehensible in the eyes of some, under the terms of Article 5, II, of Constitution.

In the case of a repentance or contractual breach during pregnancy, the situation may become even more complex. Under a strict legal definition of person, the embryo or pre-embryo cannot be considered a person. However, they also do not fit into a definition of property, because they cannot be disposed of in any situation, and neither party has exclusive rights over them. This conclusion shows that when it comes to embryos, legal rights are not exact. Thus, it can be said that embryos are somewhere between the definitions of person and property.[27]

It should be noted that, even if the surrogacy contract – whether free or onerous – is considered valid, the core of its object is the establishment of filiation (on the one hand, the surrogate promises that she will deliver the child; on the other hand, the intended parents promise to pay the agreed price – in the event of a pecuniary contract – and register the child in the name of both parents). Any question relating to minor children must have as a guiding vector the best interest of the child born or to be born, which should be weighed next to the good faith of the contract and the prohibition of the *venire contra factum proprium*.

5. Child-raising contracts

The possibility of an arrangement or a contract between people for the generation of children has been recognized for some time now. It is a materialization of absolute dissociation of sexuality and parenthood, based on logic that motherhood and paternity are functions that may be completely separated from conjugality. In this scenario, the marriage –

27 See ERICKSON, Thereza M.; ERICKSON, Megan T. "What happens to embryos when a marriage dissolves? Embryo disposition and divorce", *In: William Mitchell Law Review*, vol. 35, Issue 2, pp. 469- 488, 2009, p. 481.

sex – reproduction tripod remains completely altered and the exercise of parenting ceases to be a consequence of the loving relationship of the child 's parents. As Rodrigo da Cunha Pereira warns, there are people who only want to establish a life in common with another, but do not want to have children. And there are others who wish to have their offspring without establishing a marital bond.[28]

With the revolution brought about by ART two people can have a child without even touching each other. They meet, go to a clinic or human reproduction center, choose one of the techniques and can exercise parenting without major obstacles, either in terms of access to techniques or in terms of establishing filiation at a later time.

The complexities of these agreements arise when more than two people build this parental project. For example, a gay couple and a lesbian couple, where one of the women would have a child of one of the men. It should be noted that, although there is no doubt about the genetic motherhood and fatherhood of this child, the parental project was thought by 4 people. Probably the child will habitually live with one of the couples and spend seasons with the other couple. Or both couples may have shared custody of the child. The emerging issues: In the event that the legal and genetic mother of the child dies, the child automatically moves in with the biological father (who is the surviving parent), without considering that he has always lived with his mother and her partner or wife? If the infant's genetic father dies, is his partner or husband left without any right or duty to the child? Will it be an obstacle to frequent visits and coexistence from one hour to the next?

In order for all parties to have their parental rights recognized, it is still necessary to seek justice for the recognition of a legal multiple parenthood, which represents a breakdown of paradigms in Family Law, based on a binary logic. Such a contract, even if it is not enforceable in court could serve as a strong proof of the intent of the persons involved and help to clarify the child's best interest in the concrete case.

28 PEREIRA, Rodrigo da Cunha. *Dicionário de direito de família e sucessões*, cit., p. 184.

6. Conclusion

Artificial reproduction is a scientific development that invokes a multitude of ethical and legal considerations, with various social, religious and political nuances. Several decades after the birth of the first child of ART, few places in the world have comprehensive and clear laws on the establishment of the children's affiliation originated by these techniques. Brazil, although dealing with the subject in the Civil Code, did it in an insufficient way, a fact that finds justification in the social understanding of family and the technologies existing at the time of elaboration of the project of the Code, in the decade of 1970.

As evidenced in the course of the study, the Resolutions of the Federal Medical Council do not replace the law, nor even have a supplementary character, constituting merely deontological guidelines that bind only doctors and health services. The social and juridical notion of the family advanced, assisted reproduction techniques progressed vertiginously. Legislation is needed to frame this reality. Existing legislation, with all possible adaptations, extensive interpretations and analogies that can be made, does not provide answers to all the questions that arise in this matter.

Many children are born every year from ART in Brazil. In recent times, the techniques have been open to both female and male homosexual couples, with the possibility of shared gestation and surrogacy. But Family Law did not keep pace with this advance. For example, the Brazilian Civil Code determines a presumption of filiation of the mother's husband. But can the *pater is est* presumption be extended to the father's husband? What about *mater semper certa est* presumption in a logic of surrogacy and gestation by couples of lesbians where, as a rule, the mother who will carry the child in her womb and the woman who donated the egg are different people?

Given the current state of understanding of filiation in our system (as a function and not as a biological fatality), it would be better for the presumptions of motherhood and parenthood to be directed to the "parents of intention", the authors of the parental project, regardless the sexual orientation of the couple. Thus, father and mother, in assisted reproduction, should be those who sought the resources of reproductive medicine to procreate.

The Law must adapt to the realities in force and establish that motherhood is not due to the fact of childbirth, but the desire to be a mother. Thus, in the hypothesis of assisted reproduction among lesbians, the mother should be the one who gives birth, as well as the woman who is his wife or companion, regardless of who has donated the genetic material.

Following the same reasoning, in the hypothesis of medically assisted procreation by gays, the father should be the one who donated the genetic material, as well as the man who is his husband or partner. Except in a case of *ab initio* multiple parenthood (with a parenting contract) the maternity of surrogate should be disregarded.

In the case of heterosexual couples, the presumption of paternity in relation to the husband of the mother could continue to exist, but should also be extended to the companion, provided a proof of a stable union by deed or other document with public faith.

Any state intervention in assisted human reproduction is more than desirable: it is necessary. It is preferable to create a diploma or a statute of its own, where all clinical aspects are satisfactorily and systematically regulated (there is nothing to prevent a reference to the CFM Resolution dealing with the matter or to use the text as the basis of the law to be created). There also should be dispositions on administrative, civil and criminal penalties for the use of ART. As mentioned, lawmakers have been systematically indolent in this area, and certainly this is not a good strategy. This delay has left a legal void in a booming area with practices that have flourished and flowed into an unregulated market where frauds and abuses end up neglected. The Resolution of the Federal Council of Medicine ends up offering only a false sense of legal certainty.

In fact, there are no rules and restrictions, other than those of a deontological character created by CFM itself, which do not bind any person other than doctors and health services. Brazil ended up making feasible a medical system for coping with infertility and promoting parenthood, but forgot to legally legitimize the practice, a fact recognized even by CFM itself. It is inconceivable that such a matter – of public order – is left to autonomous bodies and without legislative competence, in a kind of extra-juridical self-regulation.

The National Congress should create a national policy that obliges everyone – doctors, patients, lawyers – to think critically about the social, family, medical and legal implications of assisted reproduction techniques, which are already deeply rooted among us. Only then, once a regulatory structure with executive force is adopted,

Brazilian families that use ART can be confident about all the legal effects resulting from the use of techniques.

In the context of such labyrinthine and complex situations, with evident reflections in the most diverse spheres of life of the parties, it is necessary that the law offer safe and unequivocal paths for all. In other words, a legislative adjustment of the rights, obligations and protections of the various actors in the process of assisted reproduction is essential in order to safeguard one of the most sublime projects in people's lives. Finally, ART protection system should be based on an idea of procreative and family pluralism, in compliance with the constitutional commandments of the dignity of the human person, equality, freedom; family diversity and fence of social retrogression.

7. References

BARON, Noah; BAZZELL, Jennifer. "Assisted Reproductive Technologies", *In: Georgetown Journal of Gender and the Law*, Vol. 15, n. 1, pp. 57-94, 2014.

CAHN, Naomi R. *Test tube families:* why the fertility market needs regulation. New York/London: New York University Press, 2009.

CHAVES, Marianna. *Homoafetividade e direito:* proteção constitucional, uniões, casamento e parentalidade. 2. ed. Curitiba: Juruá, 2012.

CRUZ, Myrel Marin. "Diagnostico Genetico Preimplantacional: Consideraciones Juridicas del Uso de Embriones Pre-Seleccionados para Evitar Condiciones Geneticas", *In: Revista Juridica Universidad de Puerto Rico*, Vol. 82, n. 1, pp. 249-266, 2013.

DANTAS, Eduardo. *Direito médico.* 3 ed. Rio de Janeiro: GZ, 2014.

ERICKSON, Thereza M.; ERICKSON, Megan T. "What happens to embryos when a marriage dissolves? Embryo disposition and divorce", *In: William Mitchell Law Review*, vol. 35, Issue 2, pp. 469- 488, 2009.

GLENNON, Theresa. "Choosing One: Resolving the Epidemic of Multiples in Assisted Reproduction", *In: Villanova Law Review* , Vol. 55, n. 1, pp. 147-204, 2010.

KATZ, Gregory; SCHWEITZER, Stuart O. "Implications of Genetic Testing for Health Policy", *In: Yale Journal of Health Policy, Law, and Ethics*, Vol. 10, n. 1, pp. 90-134, 2010.

KING, Jaime S. "And Genetic Testing for All – The Coming Revolution in Non-Invasive Prenatal Genetic Testing", *In: Rutgers Law Journal*, Vol. 42, n. 3, pp. 599-658, 2011.

MUTCHERSON, Kimberly M. "Procreative pluralism", *In: Berkeley Journal of Gender, Law & Justice*, Vol. 30, n. 1, pp. 22-75, 2015.

______. "Transformative Reproduction", *In: Journal of Gender, Race & Justice*, Vol. 16, n. 1, pp. 187-234, 2013.

GARRISON, Marsha. "Law Making for Baby Making: An Interpretive Approach to the Determination of Legal Parentage", *In: Harvard Law Review*, Vol. 113, n. 4, pp. 835-923, 2000.

NAMBA, Edison Tetsuzo. "Direito à identidade genética ou direito ao reconhecimento das origens e a reprodução assistida heteróloga", *In: Doutrinas essenciais* – Família e sucessões: direito de família/ Yussef Said Cahali; Francisco José Cahali (Orgs.). São Paulo: Editora Revista dos Tribunais, pp. 1385-1406, 2011.

NEVES, M. Patrão. "PMA: do desejo de um filho ao filho desejado", *In: Separata de Do início ao fim da vida* – Actas do Colóquio de Bioética. Braga: Faculdade de Filosofia da Universidade Católica Portuguesa, pp. 113-137, 2005.

OLIVEIRA, Guilherme de. "Aspectos jurídicos da procriação assistida", in: *Temas de Direito da Medicina*/ Guilherme de Oliveira. 2. ed. Coimbra: Coimbra Editora, pp. 5-30, 2005.

______. "Legislar sobre Procriação Assistida", in: *Temas de Direito da Medicina*/ Guilherme de Oliveira. 2. ed. Coimbra: Coimbra Editora, pp. 89-104, 2005.

PEREIRA, Rodrigo da Cunha. *Dicionário de direito de família e sucessões*: ilustrado. São Paulo: Saraiva, 2015.

PREISLER, Andrea. "Assisted Reproductive Technology: The Dangers of an Unregulated Market and the Need for Reform", *In: DePaul Journal of Health Care Law*, Vol. 15, n. 2, pp. 213-236, 2013.

RAPOSO, Vera Lúcia. *De mãe para mãe*: questões legais e éticas suscitadas pela maternidade de substituição. Coimbra: Coimbra, 2005.

______. "Direitos reprodutivos", *In: Lex Medicinae* – Revista Portuguesa de Direito da Saúde. Ano 2, n. 3. Coimbra: Centro de Direito Biomédico/ Coimbra Editora, pp. 111-131, 2005.

______. "Pode trazer o menu, por favor? Quero escolher o meu embrião – Os múltiplos casos de selecção de embriões em sede de diagnóstico genético pré-implantação", *In: Lex Medicinae* – Revista Portuguesa de Direito da Saúde, Ano 4, n. 8, pp. 59-84, 2007.

REIS, Rafael Vale e. "Responsabilidade penal na procriação medicamente assistida – A criminalização do recurso à maternidade de substituição e outras opções legais duvidosas", *In: Lex Medicinae* – Revista Portuguesa de Direito da Saúde, Ano 7, n. 13, pp. 69-93, 2010.

SAPKO, Vera Lucia da Silva. *Do direito à paternidade e maternidade dos homossexuais*: sua viabilização pela adoção e reprodução assistida. Curitiba: Juruá, 2005.

SHIVAKUMAR, Pryianka. "Count Your Chickens before They Hatch – How Multiple Pregnancies Are Endangering the Right to Abortion", *In: Brooklyn Law Review*, Vol. 78, n. 1, pp. 201-230, 2012.

SILVA, José Afonso da. *Comentário contextual à Constituição*. 5. ed. São Paulo: Malheiros Editores, 2008.

SILVESTRE, Margarida. *Embriões excedentários:* entre a técnica, a lei e a ética. Coimbra: Coimbra Editora, 2015.

Impressão e acabamento:
Grupo Smart Printer
Soluções em impressão